In this book a leading contemporary theologian investigates the relation between religion and society. Professor Davis begins with the thesis that society is a product of human agency; this raises immediately the questions of the meaning of modernity and of the function of religion in that context. The linguistic and pragmatic orientation of modern philosophy and social theory leads to a discussion of religious language and of *praxis*. Whether modernity is an incomplete project, as Habermas would have it, or a mistaken universalism, as the post-moderns maintain, is debated under the heading of human identity, both individual and collective, and in an examination of the formation of the modern self. The practical relevance of the theoretical analyses comes to the fore in a critique of Michael Novak's attempt to make 'democratic capitalism' an ideal. Professor Davis shows that, paradoxically, the post-modern rejection of secularity can be interpreted as a return from the secular to the supernatural.

RELIGION AND THE MAKING OF SOCIETY

CAMBRIDGE STUDIES IN IDEOLOGY AND RELIGION

Religion increasingly is seen as a renewed force, and is recognised as an important factor in the modern world in all aspects of life – cultural, economic, and political. It is no longer a matter of surprise to find religious factors at work in areas and situations of political tension. However, our information about these situations has tended to come from two main sources. The news-gathering agencies are well-placed to convey information, but are hampered by the fact that their representatives are not equipped to provide analysis of the religious forces involved. Alternatively, the movements generate their own accounts, which understandably seem less than objective to outside observers. There is no lack of information or factual material, but a real need for sound academic analysis. 'Cambridge Studies in Ideology and Religion' will meet this need. It will give an objective, balanced, and programmatic coverage to issues which – while of wide potential interest – have been largely neglected by analytical investigation, apart from the appearance of sporadic individual studies. Intended to enable debate to proceed at a higher level, the series should lead to a new phase in our understanding of the relationship between ideology and religion.

RELIGION AND THE MAKING OF SOCIETY

Essays in social theology

CHARLES DAVIS

Emeritus Professor of Religion,
Concordia University, Montreal

CAMBRIDGE
UNIVERSITY PRESS

Published by the Press Syndicate of the University of Cambridge
The Pitt Building, Trumpington Street, Cambridge CB2 1RP
40 West 20th Street, New York, NY 10011-4211, USA
10 Stamford Road, Oakleigh, Melbourne 3166, Australia

First published 1994

Printed in Great Britain at the University Press, Cambridge

A catalogue record for this book is available from the British Library

Library of Congress cataloguing in publication data

Davis, Charles, 1923–
Religion and the making of society: essays in social theology / Charles Davis.
p.   cm. – (Cambridge studies in ideology and religion)
Includes bibliographical references and index.
ISBN 0 521 44310 5 (hardback) – ISBN 0 521 44789 5 (paperback)
1. Sociology, Christian.   2. Religion and sociology.
3. Religion and politics.   4. Ideology – Religious aspects.
I. Title.   II. Series.
BT738.D36   1994
261 – dc20   93–10224 CIP

ISBN 0 521 44310 5 hardback
ISBN 0 521 44789 5 paperback

For my son Anthony

Contents

General editors' preface   *page* xi
Acknowledgements   xiii

Introduction: from the secular to the supernatural   1

PART I   Society, religion and human agency

1   Society and the critique of modernity   21

2   The present social function of religion   39

3   From inwardness to social action: the
    transformation of the political   48

4   The Christian question to radicalism   63

PART II   *Praxis*, narrative and religious language

5   Theology and *praxis*   77

6   Revelation, historical continuity and the
    rationality of tradition   96

7   The political use and misuse of religious
    language   112

PART III   From the modern subject to the post-
           modern self

8   Our new religious identity   131

9   Post-modernity and the formation of the self   153

ix

PART IV   The option for the future

10   What remains of socialism as a moral and
     religious ideal   173

11   Communicative rationality and the grounding
     of religious hope   188

Index   206

General editors' preface

Only twenty years ago it was widely assumed that religion had lost its previous place in Western culture and that this pattern would spread throughout the world. Since then religion has become a renewed force, recognized as an important factor in the modern world in all aspects of life, cultural, economic and political. This is true not only of the Third World, but in Europe East and West, and in North America. It is no longer a surprise to find a religious factor at work in areas of political tension.

Religion and ideology. form a mixture which can be of interest to the observer, but in practice dangerous and explosive. Our information about such matters comes for the most part from three types of sources. The first is the media which understandably tend to concentrate on newsworthy events, without taking the time to deal with the underlying issues of which they are but symptoms. The second source comprises studies by social scientists who often adopt a functionalist and reductionist view of the faith and beliefs which motivate those directly involved in such situations. Finally, there are the statements and writings of those committed to the religious or ideological movements themselves. We seldom lack information, but there is a need – often an urgent need – for sound objective analysis which can make use of the best contemporary approaches to both politics and religion. 'Cambridge Studies in Ideology and Religion' is designed to meet this need.

The subject matter is global and this will be reflected in the choice both of topics and authors. The initial volumes will be concerned primarily with movements involving the Christian religion, but as the series becomes established movements involving other world religions will be subjected to the same objective critical analysis. In all cases it is our intention that an accurate and sensitive account of religion should be informed by an objective and sophisticated application of perspectives from the social sciences.

Christian social theology has in recent days been going through a period of turbulence and re-assessment. For a variety of reasons older approaches to the subject seem no longer to be valid. Marxism and various brands of socialism are no longer monopolizing the role of dialogue partner with social theology. There have been a number of interesting encounters with neo-conservative thinking and with other religions, together with a new concern for the foundations of the discipline. In all this, Charles Davis has been one of the most creative and stimulating thinkers. This book of essays will provide stimulus and illumination to all who are interested in the relationship between theology and the social sciences, and the social relevance of theology.

DUNCAN FORRESTER AND ALISTAIR KEE
New College, University of Edinburgh

Acknowledgements

My first thanks must go to my wife, Florence, without whose collaboration this book would not have come to a successful birth.

Thanks are also due to those who gave permission to use material previously published elsewhere. 'Religion and the making of society', reprinted by special permission of Northwestern University School of Law, *Northwestern University Law Review*, 81/4 (1987), pp. 718–31, and of Cambridge University Press; 'The end of religion', *Compass*, 6/1 (1988), pp. 6–9; 'From inwardness to social action: a shift in the locus of religious experience', *New Blackfriars*, 67/789 (March 1986), 114–25; 'The political use and misuse of religious language', *Journal of Ecumenical Studies*, 26/3 (Summer 1989), pp. 482–95; 'Our new religious identity', *SR: Studies in Religion/Sciences Religieuses*, 9/1 (Winter 1980), pp. 25–39. Copyright held by Canadian Corporation for Studies in Religion. 'Our modern identity: the formation of the self', *Modern Theology*, 6/2 (January 1990), pp. 159–71; 'Theology and praxis', *Crosscurrents*, 23/2 (Summer 1973), pp. 154–71; 'The limits of politics: the Christian clash with radicalism', in *Cities of Gods: Faith, Politics and Pluralism in Judaism, Christianity and Islam*, ed. Nigel Biggar, James S. Scott, William Schweiker (Westport, CT: Greenwood Publishing Group, 1986), 143–50; 'What remains of socialism as a moral and religious ideal' was read as a paper at the conference *Religion and the Resurgence of Capitalism*, held at Lancaster, England, 14–17 July 1991 and will be published in the volume, *Theology, Ethics and Resurgent Capitalism*, resulting from that conference. I thank Professor Richard H. Roberts, organizer and editor for permission to include it also in this book. 'Communicative rationality and the grounding of religious hope' has been published in a German translation by Edmund Arens in *Habermas und die Theologie*, ed. Edmund Arens (Patmos: Düsseldorf, 1989), pp. 96–115. This is the first publication in English.

The Introduction and Chapters 6 and 11 are being published here for the first time.

Introduction: from the secular to the supernatural

The purpose of this book is to investigate the relation between religion and society. It begins by examining the thesis that society is the product of human agency. That thesis is characteristic of the modern period. Hence it immediately raises the question of the meaning of modernity and the function of religion within the modern context (Chapters 1–4). The linguistic and pragmatic orientations of both modern philosophy and social theory lead to a discussion of narrative and social practice as vehicles of meaning (Chapters 5–7). The question whether modernity is an incomplete project, as Jürgen Habermas would have it, or a mistaken universalism, as the post-moderns maintain, is debated under the heading of our identity, both individual and collective, and in an examination of the formation of the modern self (Chapters 8–9). The practical relevance of the theoretical analyses comes to the fore in a critique of Michael Novak's suggestion that we make 'democratic capitalism' our ideal, and in an original attempt to define religious hope and its grounding in terms of communicative rationality (Chapters 10–11).

This introduction has a threefold function. First, to introduce the themes developed in the sequence of chapters. Second, to supplement the discussion as found in the chapters by bringing into the discussion some very recent material, particularly the work of John Milbank and his surprising use of the Catholic philosopher, Maurice Blondel. Third, to outline the general context within which all the particular discussions take place, namely, a shift in theology from a focus upon the secular and the theology of secularization to a focus upon the supernatural and the theology of grace or of supernatural liberation. Paradoxically enough that change in the focus of theology bears some significant similarity with the much talked about transition from modernity to post-modernity. That similarity might be fruitfully exploited by theology.

Religion is a form of social practice. It is therefore affected by the manner in which society is conceived and organized. Secularization is one particular way of conceiving and organizing society. A secular society is a society or people that has not committed itself as a collectivity to a single set of ultimate beliefs and values. It is pluralist in the sense that it embraces people who differ in regard to their adherence to ultimate beliefs and values. A secular, pluralist society is not secularist in the sense of embodying an ideology hostile to religion.

A secular society arose in the West with the transition of modernity. Indeed, the coming of a secular society is one of the defining features of modernity. Underlying secular society is a prior conception that society is not given anterior to human freedom but is a human construction. According to the pre-modern conception, society was part of the cosmic order. Human beings had to conform to the necessary laws of the social order. A false necessity restricted human freedom within boundaries unchangeable by human action. In the words of Roberto Unger, quoted and elaborated in the first chapter, 'society is an artifact'. As I argue there I do not find the formulation used by Unger a happy one. 'Artifact' relates the construction of society to instrumental and technical reason. A more balanced view of the making of society would stress the contribution of substantive reason and the role of virtue.

The insight that society is a human construct is not the only feature that distinguishes modern society from pre-modern society. Pre-modern society was an undifferentiated whole. In the Christian Middle Ages the Church was the total society. It absorbed all political and socio-cultural elements into itself. A secular, pluralist society was unthinkable. Paradoxically enough the first differentiation of that total society into a duality of Church and State was the result of the papal victory in the Investiture controversy. The victory of Pope Gregory VII in excluding the Emperor from ecclesiastical investitures caused the first separation of State from Church. The Emperor as Emperor was now thrust out of the Church, and the Empire became a secular reality. It was not fully secular in the modern sense because of the higher dominion claimed by the Church, but it was the first step in freeing the political sphere as secular.

The history of the West is that of a progressive differentiation between Church and State, between religion and society. The radical change came as a result of the Religious Wars which followed the Reformation. The seventeenth century saw the full emergence of the State as secular, that is, the legitimation of its power structure without any appeal to the Christian religion. Apart from the differentiation of Church and State, of religion and culture, the process of differentiation affected other functions of society. The economic sphere established itself as an autonomous realm, allowing only economic factors to guide economic policy and decisions. But if modern society consists of autonomous yet interrelated spheres of meaning and action, what is the function of religion? Is religion outside the social order or does it still have a function? It is the argument of the recent book by Marcel Gauchet, *Le Désenchantement du monde: Une histoire politique de la religion* (Paris: Gallimard, 1986), examined in Chapter 2, that religion as a structural principle of society has come to an end. Christianity came on the scene as the 'religion of the exit from religion', and the Christian religion came to an end around 1700. When Gauchet speaks of religion he limits its meaning to religion as a social system. He does not deny that religion as a reality outside the social order still has validity. It follows from his thesis that 'religion' in its purest form, namely as a social system, came at the beginning in primitive religion. For him, then, 'religion' in the strict sense means that way of thinking and acting which presupposes that society with its structure is given prior to human agency and is therefore unchangeable.

Gauchet's thesis may be seen as an idiosyncratic version of the theology of secularization. In broad terms, the theology of secularization is an attempt to give a positive assessment of

modern secular society by interpreting that society as the
legitimate outcome of the Christian faith itself. When the
modern world emerged at the beginning of the fifteenth
century it met with opposition from the Church. Secular
society was identified with hostility to religion. What remained
as the ideal was the restoration of Christendom. However, a
shift of attitude took place a few decades ago. It was argued
that the granting of a relative autonomy to the secular enterprise need not be interpreted as a rebellion, but simply a
differentiation between the sacred and the secular. The most
outstanding Protestant theologian of secularization is Gogarten. On the Catholic side the *locus classicus* is the document
Gaudium et Spes of the Second Vatican Council, together with
the political theology of J. B. Metz. Essential to the theology of
secularization is a duality between the world and faith or grace,
and an acknowledgement of the autonomy of the world.
Gauchet, however, takes an extreme position in interpreting
the relation of religion to society. According to him, modern
religion, or religion after secularization, is not in any way a
structural principle of society. He rejects completely the idea
that the social order has a source outside itself. It is in no way
due to a religious or sacred agency. This seems to me to imply
an extreme privatization of religion. Because, according to
Gauchet, religion understood as a social system has come to an
end, religion in the wider sense of transcendent experience
becomes entirely subjective. As a social factor, it relates to
society only as a subjective, critical principle. This thesis is in
strong contrast to Metz's political theology which understands
its task as a deprivatization.

The problem, then, is the respective roles of human agency
and religion in the making of society. Does one exclude the
other? If society is seen as a human artifact or construction,
does that exclude a recognition of the intervention of a transcendent principle? On the other hand, if society is seen as the
result of a revelation or supernatural principle, does that
exclude human agency so that society is entirely a sacral
structure or a theocracy?

Much here depends upon how one conceives religious experience. Harm has been done in conceiving religious faith and practice in too narrow a manner. In Chapter 3 I argue for a much wider concept of religious experience than is usually operative in dealing with the social and political functions of religion. There are three places in the whole gamut of human experience where we find a mediation of transcendent experience. These are the cognitive, the normative and the expressive. In each of these places religious experience takes on a distinctive form. In the cognitive sphere, we find cosmic religion; in the normative, political religion; in the expressive, contemplative religion. An important thesis underlying that typology of religious experience is that there is no distinctively religious sphere. Religious faith and practice is a dimension of human experience in all its forms. To think otherwise is a form of idolatry, because it fails to acknowledge that religion is found only when human experience is transcended.

One approach to the secular would be to see it as the acknowledgement of change. Gauchet interprets religion as the idea that the social order comes from a source outside human agency and is thus already given as immutable prior to human freedom and activity. In contrast to the sacred unchangeableness characteristic of religion, the secular, in seeing the social order as due to human agency, implies the acknowledgement of the changeableness of every social order. But even granted that the social order is the result of human creativity there are limits to that creativity. In Chapter 4 I have argued that there is a clash between radicalism and orthodox Christianity. By radicalism I understand the claim that human agency can fundamentally change the human condition. The radicals are those who think that human reason and will are powerful enough to overcome the present, imperfect human condition by bringing about social and political change. Traditionally, human beings have appealed to religion and its transcendent principles for consolation in the face of the aporias of human existence. Generally, those who reject religion declare that human beings must learn to live without consolation when confronted by death and other negativities. The question, however, remains: how far can we reform the social order? What are the limits of social revolution? If we try fundamentally to change the present social order are we not in danger of making things worse instead of better?

In general terms it can be said that the context for theology since the seventeenth century has been secular. Even though until this century the Church opposed the modern secular world, a duality of Church and world, of sacred and secular, nevertheless determined theological reflection. Despite the open hostility of Church to the world, some of the principles characteristic of secularity found their way into theology, such as the priority of knowledge over love, the positivisitic concept of reason, the search for certitude and necessary laws, the stress on identity instead of otherness and plurality. The last phase of theology's dalliance with the rationalism of the Enlightenment was the theology of secularization, which freed the secular to do its own thing without any check from the supernatural.

Paradoxically enough, a new context is emerging for theology: post-modernity with its emphasis upon contingency, the particular, difference, narrativity and fallibility. In other words, there is a return to the supernatural. John Milbank writes against the secular order in his book *Theology and Social Theory*, of which the subtitle is *Beyond Secular Reason*.[1] In the chapter on Liberation Theology he cites the work of Maurice Blondel as providing a sound understanding of the supernatural in relation to the social and political order.

Does in fact the thought of Blondel offer theologians the possibility of moving from a dominating secular framework to an overtly supernatural context without returning to traditional, pre-modern modes of thought? To assess Milbank's claim that it does, we need to set forth the main lines of Blondel's thought, which will be done here in the Introduction. We will return to Blondel at the end of Chapter 5 in order to relate his 'pragmatism' to the discussions on theory and *praxis*.

The *chef d'œuvre* of Blondel is *L'Action* (1893). He later expanded this in a multi-volume series, but the earlier volume,

[1] John Milbank, *Theology and Social Theory: Beyond Secular Reason* (Oxford: Blackwell, 1990).

which was his doctoral dissertation, remains normative for understanding his thought. What Blondel gives us is a dialectic of action. Action is all specifically human activity. He follows a method of implication in which he studied action, not in what it has of contingence, but in what it has of necessity. There is, he maintains, a dialectic that was necessary and immanent to human life. He made a distinction between *volonté voulante* and *volonté voulue*. The first, *volonté voulante*, is the underlying principle of voluntary action, the deep aspiration of the human will; the second, *volonté voulue*, is any particular object of a precise, determining act of will. The dynamic of the dialectic is to make the *volonté voulue* adequate to the *volonté voulante*. The dialectic set forth in *L'Action* aims at revealing the series of ends which the will cannot but will. The problem posed by Blondel is the relation between autonomy and heteronomy. For him this problem was solved by the supernatural. Human beings achieved their autonomy by surrendering themselves to God.

Blondel establishes his thesis in detail by an analysis of the various levels of human action. The setting forth of the levels or stages of human action is rich in psychological insights that allow us to see Blondel as a precursor of the existentialists. But it is not the aim of Blondel to give psychological descriptions. His concern is to uncover the logic of human action, using a regressive analysis. He begins with two preliminary attitudes which would evade the challenge of human destiny. The first of these attitudes is dilettantism. The dilettante refuses to take any question concerning the meaning of life seriously. If the dilettante attempts to avoid the problem of human destiny by refusing to will anything, the nihilist wills nothingness. Nihilism is the second attitude that attempts to evade the challenge of human destiny. The dilettante does not will anything: the nihilist wills nothing. But neither attitude can escape the dynamic thrust present in the depths of the human will.

After having disposed of these two attempts at evasion, Blondel examines the positive solutions to the problem of human action. Under the heading 'the phenomenon of action' Blondel analyses the various values for which men and women live and die. In doing so he distinguishes the series of stages related so as to constitute the logic of human action. Each stage in the dialectic is found to be insufficient in itself, so that if we follow the logic of human action, uncovering the implications of each stage, we shall be forced to transcend each stage in a process of seeking a higher unity. Blondel's analysis moves through the following stages: from objective science to the science of the subject, from consciousness to voluntary action, from intentional effort to the exterior expansion of action, from individual to social action, from social action to superstitious action. Superstition refers to any merely human attempt to satisfy an infinite need for an absolute. Throughout this ascent the human will in its depth has been seeking to find something that would complete it as its term. Superstition is the last attempt to make phenomena suffice. The attempt is a failure. The attempt of human beings to be self-sufficient does not and cannot succeed. To fulfil the aspiration of the *volonté voulante* human beings must turn to the Unique Necessary Being. Thus, human beings to fulfil themselves must turn to what is beyond themselves. Science and art, language and work, are not just expressions of human creativity, they are phenomena that in their implications uncover the social nature of the human agent. Further, society is not an absolute, but it is governed by laws and principles rooted in the Absolute or the Unique Necessary Being. Until he reaches the Absolute, Blondel does not attribute full ontological reality to the phenomena of the lower stages. Once he has reached the Absolute his analysis is complemented with a synthesis. Once God is affirmed the whole series of phenomena is seen as grounded in the Unique Necessary Being. In his affirmation of God Blondel rejects naturalism. Without God the natural order is unfounded. Uncircumscribed within the limits of nature God is called a supernatural being, although that use of the word 'supernatural' is obsolete in theology.

In theology since the High Middle Ages, the word 'supernatural' refers not to beings but to grace as elevating human beings to participate in the divine life. God offers human beings a destiny that lies beyond the potentiality of human nature as such. It is a free gift from God. It opens for human beings a destiny that lies beyond anything that could be regarded as demanded as proportionate to the exigencies, not only of human beings but of any finite creatures.

The dialectic of human action does not stop with the affirmation of God as the Unique Necessary Being. It pushes beyond that to force us to accept as our destiny a life that exceeds our human capacity and is of a divine order. It is here that the problem of autonomy and heteronomy reaches its most acute form. We are unable to move of ourselves towards our own destiny. Blondel meets the problem by seeing a demand or desire for supernatural grace as present in the dialectic of human action.

This was the aspect of Blondel's thought that caused the greatest controversy. It was a question of the gratuity of grace. The Scholastic concept of the supernatural was what surpasses the proper exigencies and powers of the whole of pre-existing created nature. The aim of this definition was to protect the gratuity of grace. The life of grace was supernatural because it was beyond the exigencies and powers of human nature, indeed, of any conceivable finite nature. Blondel recognized clearly that the life of grace and our supernatural destiny were beyond human power. At the same time he claimed that his method of immanence or regressive analysis uncovered a necessity or demand for a supernatural destiny. In an oft-quoted sentence: 'Absolutely impossible and absolutely necessary, that is the proper notion of the supernatural'.[2] Blondel did not deny that our supernatural destiny was contingent upon a free decree of God. The necessity in question did not mean that God was compelled to raise human beings to a supernatural order. Blondel's point was that the dialectic of human action drove human beings to form the hypothesis of a transcendent fulfilment of human aspiration. That was as far as philosophy could go. Whether God, in fact, has called human beings to a share in the divine life beyond the powers and exigencies of their nature can be affirmed only by faith.

[2] Maurice Blondel, *Action (1893): Essay on a Critique of Life and the Science of Practice*, trans. Oliva Blanchette (Notre Dame, IN: University of Notre Dame Press, 1984), p. 375.

The supernatural is, therefore, a dialectical necessity, in so far as it is seen to be an implication of human action when that is analysed. The dialectic is both unitive and dynamic. The dynamism of the ascent is called forth by the insufficiency of each stage. That insufficiency drives the human being to seek a higher unity. In Blondel the dialectic moves beyond the affirmation of God to the hypothesis of a supernatural destiny. The necessary idea of the supernatural places human beings before an alternative. They must either accept the higher vocation to which God calls them or refuse that call and in doing so close themselves off from God. There is a limit to human autonomy and, paradoxically enough, human beings can realize their limited autonomy only by surrendering them-selves to the transcendent will of God.

Blondel tried to combine the freedom and transcendence of God's gift of grace with his method of immanence, which, he claimed, revealed the innermost depths of the human will. But is the application by Blondel of his method of immanence to grace and the supernatural compatible with traditional teach-ing? Three interpretations of Blondel have been put forward. The first interprets Blondel as giving a metaphysics of human nature as such. Hence, he is maintaining that there is exigency for grace in human nature; this is incompatible with ortho-doxy. The second interpretation understands Blondel's analysis as a metaphysics of historical humanity; this is compatible with orthodox teaching on the gratuity of grace. The third interpre-tation does not limit Blondel's analysis to historical humanity. He wanted to construct a universally valid metaphysics of the human being. The object of his analysis was human beings as destined to a supernatural end.

The theological controversy concerning the gratuity of grace focused upon the hypothetical state of pure nature. If God had not called humankind to a supernatural destiny, human beings would have lived in a state proportionate to human nature as such. Properly speaking this state of pure nature is a limit concept. It simply expresses in another way that God was under no necessity to raise human beings to the supernatural order. Unfortunately some theologians thought they were justified in elaborating the details of the hypothetical state as if it were or had been a concrete reality. When he wrote *L'Action* the concept of pure nature lay outside Blondel's purview. In his later writings he gave it a place.

De Lubac leads those theologians who reject the concept of pure nature as meaningless. The concrete finality of the spirit, he contends, is constitutive of the being of that spirit. Hence, even prior to the elevation by grace, the finality of human beings, as they are, to the supernatural is constitutive of their being, intrinsic to them. The object of Blondel's study is spirit as it exists in reality. This must include its destiny to a given end. The concept of pure nature is unacceptable. It comes from a different philosophy, a philosophy that supposes that it is possible to grasp the essence of a spirit without reference to its real end. *L'Action* studies the human being as destined to the supernatural.

The hypothesis of a state of pure nature has become a *bête noire* to some theologians, and their rejection of it is too sweeping in my opinion. John Milbank regards its rejection as constitutive of integralism. He is right if one supposes that there are two complete and separate orders, the natural order and the supernatural order. I agree with him that 'every person has already been worked upon by divine grace, with the consequence that one cannot analytically separate "natural" and "supernatural" contributions to this integral unity'.[3] But it is an exaggeration to suppose that there can be no distinction between the levels of nature and grace. To illustrate this by a similar distinction. It is impossible to separate the contribution of material nature from the modifications brought about by human beings during the course of centuries. Is there anywhere where we can find untouched, virginal material nature? But that does not mean that we cannot distinguish levels of being and activity. Nature and grace are inextricably entwined. There is only one concrete order. But this order includes within itself elements of differing ontological status. Surely, the very purpose of Blondel's analysis is to take us through a series of

[3] *Theology and Social Theory*, p. 206.

stages, first in a phenomenology, which when it reaches the Absolute becomes an ontology of concrete reality as mediated through action.

This account of Blondel was introduced to show how the context of theology has changed. The presuppositions of the Enlightenment no longer fit comfortably with some of the major assumptions of more recent theology. Some of these assumptions are the priority of practice, the refusal of a single system of truth, perspectivism, fallibilism, and so on. A clear account of the assumptions and theses of a post-modern theology is to be found in an article by Milbank, 'Postmodern critical Augustinianism: a short *Summa* in forty-two responses to unasked questions'.[4] His thought is further developed in articles and in *Theology and Social Theory*. For him the secular social sciences are a bastard form of theology – a heretical theology, as it were. The eagerness of some theologians to incorporate modern secular social theory into theology is misplaced, Milbank argues. Modern theology has already swallowed more social science than is good for it, and on the other hand, modern secular social theory is more dependent upon theological assumptions than social sciences are prepared to admit.

There is undoubtedly a homology between post-modern assumptions and a theology of the supernatural. The gratuity of grace implies its contingency. This is a free gift of God; it need not have been given. The order constituted by grace is a historical and eschatological order, not a metaphysical order. It finds its expression in narrative. In that order love is prior to knowledge and consequently practice comes before theory or contemplation. Since it rests upon the free response of faith, the appropriate way it is transmitted is by persuasion through rhetoric and not by dialectic or argument. Milbank sums up post-modern thought with the three words, 'perspectivism', 'pragmatism' and 'historicism'. He endeavours to place Blondel's thought in that context:

Blondel, therefore, shows that if theology embraces a more thoroughgoing perspectivism, pragmatism and historicism, it can escape from the 'modern' illusions which claim that a purely finite, immanent science (including social science) can offer an ontology, or account of 'the way things really are'. And with the removal of the discourse of metaphysics from the competence of philosophy, the possibility of a 'supernaturalizing of the natural' is more drastically opened to view than ever before within the entire Christian era. Thus Blondel, more than anyone else, points us beyond secular reason.[5]

I cannot follow Milbank in his interpretation of Blondel. I do not think Blondel would have recognized his own thought in the anti-metaphysical historicism and pragmatism which Milbank embraces. I am reminded of the exclamation of Blondel when the Abbé Denis praised *L'Action* as a superb example of Christian apologetics: *Ab amicis nostris, libera nos, Domine!*[6]

According to Milbank there is no single system of propositional truth. We cannot by argument refute theses opposed to our own. We have our story and they have theirs. It is a question of who has the better story. We can use rhetoric to persuade but not argue. I find that a disturbing prospect. Political debate is already almost exclusively a matter of rhetoric, with little in the way of argument. Is any dialectical critique of the rhetoric that pours over us to be ruled out of order? The fact that human reason is finite and belongs to this historical world does not mean that we can drop the distinction between truth and falsity, right and wrong, just and unjust. We can do more than point to what is *de facto* acceptable at a given time and place. The standards we use are immanent and embedded in particular languages, cultures, practices. That would not make us deny the transcendence of the claims they make, nor does it exclude their openness to critique. A balanced concept of reason demands that we hold in tension two apparently contradictory features: the historical, embodied, practical character of human reason and the transcendence of particularity implied by any claim to objective truth or universal morality. To find such a concept of reason has been the driving

5   Milbank, *Theology and Social Theory*, p. 219.
6   James M. Somerville, 'Maurice Blondel 1861–1949', *Thought*, 36 (1961), p. 378.

force behind the patient investigations of Habermas.[7] As for
Milbank, I cannot see how he can escape a performative
contradiction in his own work. The erudite and carefully
worked out analyses of his book do not seem to constitute
merely an exercise in rhetorical persuasion, but a closely knit
argument – an argument, therefore, to the effect that no
argument is legitimate.

Taking place, then, is a shift in the context within which
theology is carried out. The shift has been from an acceptance
of the secular to the acknowledgement that there is only one
concrete order and that is not secular but supernatural. The
all-pervasiveness of the supernatural or grace must affect our
interpretation of the relation between theory and practice and
also our analysis of religious language. In particular the
essential role of narrative in religious expression has led to a
better understanding of the essential role of narrative in all
expression and thought. Chapters 6 and 7 are devoted to these
themes.

The difference between modern and post-modern
approaches is brought to a focus in their respective accounts of
the subject: Chapters 8 and 9 cover that area of debate,
beginning with a modern account of our new religious identity
and passing to a post-modern analysis of the formation of the
self.

There are three main intellectual and political movements in
Europe and America at this time: the *praxis* philosophy to
which critical theory, including the work of Habermas,
belongs;[8] neo-conservatism; and the philosophy of the rejection of modernity and of the Enlightenment. These three
movements form the general context of theology as well as of
social and political thought.

---

[7] For a summary account of Habermas's thought on this matter, see Thomas
McCarthy, 'Introduction', in Jürgen Habermas, *The Philosophical Discourse of
Modernity* (Cambridge: Polity Press, 1987), p. x.

[8] Under '*praxis* philosophy' Habermas includes not only the different versions of
Western Marxism but also the American pragmatism of Mead and Dewey and the
analytical philosophy of Charles Taylor. See Habermas, *The Philosophical Discourse of
Modernity*, p. 394 n. 15.

Most speculative theologians are familiar now with critical theory, with the Frankfurt School stemming from Horkheimer and Adorno and embracing the wide-ranging thought of Habermas. For a recent survey see the collective volume, *Habermas, Modernity, and Public Theology*.[9] For Habermas and for those who share his basic assumptions, modernity is an incomplete project.[10] Modernity for those thinkers does not call for an abstract negation but a determinate negation which preserves and takes up its acceptable content. In other words, there must be a rejoining of the discourse of counter-Enlightenment, which was present in the Enlightenment from its beginning. As Habermas puts it, we must return to the various crossroads to rethink the path that was open but not pursued.

I take my account of the second intellectual and political movement from Habermas's essay, 'Neoconservative culture criticism in the United States and West Germany: an intellectual movement in two political cultures'.[11] According to this account neo-conservatism goes back in America to Daniel Bell's *The Cultural Contradictions of Capitalism* (1976). What Habermas calls 'the theoretically productive center of American neoconservatism' includes Daniel Bell, Peter Berger, Nathan Glazer, Seymour Martin Lipset, Robert Nisbet and Edward Shils. From the standpoint of theology I would add Michael Novak, and I should point out that Peter Berger's writings are theological in content. Habermas named the West German counterparts.

These people are open about their liberal past. They may be described as frightened liberals. 'Hence the self understanding of Irving Kristol who sees himself as a "liberal disillusioned by reality". Peter Glotz paraphrased this definition: neoconservatism is the net into which the liberal can fall when he begins to fear his own liberalism.'[12] They fear that cultural developments

---

9 Edited by Dan S. Browning and Francis Schüssler-Fiorenza (New York: Crossroads, 1992).
10 Cf. Jürgen Habermas, 'Modernity – an incomplete project', in Hal Foster, *Postmodern Culture* (London and Sydney: Pluto Press, 1983), pp. 3–15.
11 Richard J. Bernstein, ed., *Habermas and Modernity* (Cambridge, MA: MIT Press, 1985), pp. 78–94.
12 *Ibid.*, p. 79.

will undermine social and political institutions. The two main positions they adopt are anti-communism, which extends itself into a wider anti-socialism, and anti-populism, which fears the people and sees order guaranteed by power élites. Since cultural developments are blamed for an inflation of expectation and a lack of willingness to acclaim and obey, intellectuals are denounced as destructive elements in society. Habermas sees neo-conservatist criticism as mistaking the cause for the effect. A crisis which arises in the economy and State is presented as a spiritual–moral crisis. It blames cultural modernism for the burdens caused by a capitalist modernization of the economy and society. The neo-conservatives fail to distinguish the process of modernization from cultural development.

The neoconservative does not uncover the economic and social causes for the altered attitudes towards work, consumption, achievement and leisure. Consequently, he attributes all of the following – hedonism, the lack of social identification, the lack of obedience, narcissism, the withdrawal from status and achievement competition – to the domain of 'culture'. In fact, however, culture is intervening in the creation of all these problems in only a very indirect and mediated fashion. (Habermas)[13]

Michael Novak is an exemplary instance of a neo-conservative outlook. He accepts uncritically the ongoing process of a capitalist economy but sees that process as threatened by cultural protest. He does not blame capitalism for the destructive elements in our present culture. It is socialism aided and abetted by socialist intellectuals that, according to Novak, is leading to the breakdown of modern society. Hence, he sets about developing a spiritual and moral capitalist culture.

The outlook of Michael Novak corresponds to the outlook dominant among conservative church people and hierarchs. They accept more or less without question the modernization of our society, understood as the reorganization of the economy by technical reason. They are frightened by the upheaval this causes but they do not rightly discern the cause, and so they try to remedy the effects by appeals to moral and spiritual values.

[13] Foster, ed., *Postmodern Culture*, p. 7.

What they fear above all is the people and popular religion as the originating source of popular protest against the injustices brought about by capitalist economy. They see themselves as defenders of Christian values and culture, and blame the breakdown of those values in present society upon the protest-culture, the left-wing intellectuals, vaguely referred to as socialists. They ignore the destruction wrought by a market economy and the power structure to which it gives rise. We may think here of individuals like Ratzinger and movements such as Opus Dei.

The third context for theology is a theology of the departure from modernity. Here we may place the recent volume of writings by Protestant theologians on deconstructionism and theology. For example, we may mention the work of Mark C. Taylor. Here, also, we may place the work of John Milbank, an Anglican theologian. Milbank situates his own book in a post-Nietzschean context. In bidding farewell to secular reason, he is not contending for a return to a pre-modern metaphysics and theology. His thought is essentially post-modern in the rejection of a single system of truth based on universal reason.

Flechtheim,[14] a futurologist, sees us as being faced with three possible futures. Future One is a totally monetarized and bureaucratized society, a totally administered society without meaning and love. Future Two is a militaristic society continually preparing and making war. Future Three establishes a realm of freedom and reconciliation, a democratic, socialist society in which all men and women could realize their potentialities and develop materially and spiritually. The likelihood of Future Two has diminished considerably with the breakdown of state socialism in Eastern Europe. What, however, still confronts us is the choice between Future One and Future Three. The collapse of communism should not be interpreted as a simple victory for capitalism. In other words, it should not be a question of the abstract negation of communism but as a determinate negation which takes up, preserves, what is worthy of being saved. This is where theology has a role

[14] I owe this reference to an unpublished paper of Rudolf J. Siebert.

in choosing Future Three in a critique of both capitalism and state socialism.

The last chapter of this book, Chapter 12 on religious hope, returns to the question of the necessity of the supernatural. It confronts us with the aporia created for communicative rationality by the destruction of communication by death. It endeavours to show that ultimate fulfilment, the object of Christian hope, comes as a transcendent gift or grace. Because it is a gift, it is gratuitous and contingent. Hence the object of hope cannot be inferred as a fact from the immanent dynamic of human existence. It must be grounded upon a contingent event of a divine disclosure. Such a revelatory event is both necessary and contingent. It is necessary because without it there is no ultimate fulfilment corresponding to the dynamic of human existence. It is contingent because we cannot lay claim to what God gives as a free gift. It is possible that he might have left us for a lesser destiny. It is the concept of the supernatural that brings together necessity and contingency.

In moving its focus from the secular to the supernatural, theology might well find itself better able to deal with the problems raised by post-modernity.

PART I

Society, religion and human agency

CHAPTER I

Society and the critique of modernity

There is no doubt that Roberto Unger[1] has identified an insight basic to modern society and to modern social and political theory: society is an artifact. I fully endorse his attempt to consistently work out the implications of that basic insight against the constant temptation of human beings to give unconditional authority to conditional forms, thus concealing from themselves the process of imagining and making society and its institutions. Unger is right in supposing that viewing society as an artifact combines the liberal/leftist aim of freeing society from structures of dependence and domination with the modernist goal of rescuing subjectivity and intersubjectivity from rigid roles. I find no difficulty, then, in responding favourably to Unger's work as a major contribution to our thinking about society. The clarification of our freedom to reimagine and remake the social worlds which we have constructed and in which we live is undoubtedly the way forward from our present situation.

At the same time, coming to the question of society from the study of religion and the philosophy of history, I confront a series of difficulties and objections in embracing the thesis that society is an artifact. In the pages that follow I will sketch out some of these problems.

Although religion has sometimes fuelled revolution, it has

[1] This essay was first published in the *Northwestern University Law Review*, 81/4 (Summer 1987), pp. 718–31 as a contribution to a symposium on the work of Roberto Unger. The symposium, including my essay, was later published as a book: Robin W. Lovin and Michael J. Perry, eds., *Critique and Construction: A Symposium on Roberto Unger's Politics* (Cambridge: Cambridge University Press, 1990).

historically more often been a factor of social integration. It has secured the social order by declaring that order sacred (or at least of sacred origin), thus giving it what Unger would label a false necessity and a mistaken unconditionality. It is true that, in the Christian West, the frequent conflict of Church and State has forged a distinction between the sacred and the secular. Nevertheless, because the Church with its sacred institutions often legitimized and solidified the State and other parts of the social fabric, society was frequently conceived as an affair of divine ordinance rather than a product of human freedom. Unger's argument, then, poses a problem for religion: how can one free social forms from an unnecessary rigidity without denying religion a role in the making of society? Is there no relationship between the authority of the social world and the authority of ultimate reality? Must every attempt to establish a relationship be an illegitimate conferring of unconditional authority upon conditional forms.

I assume that Unger does not want to deny validity to all forms of religious faith. But any religious faith implies privileged beliefs. As a complex of symbols and as a cultural institution, religion claims in some form to provide answers to questions of ultimate meaning, questions about the nature and destiny of human beings. And religion, unlike comprehensive ideologies (such as Marxism), seeks its answers in a transcendent realm, in an appeal to some form of superhuman power. Inevitably, therefore, a religious person will hold that human life – and human society – are founded upon transempirical truths. To the religious, certain principles of faith and morality stand over the whole order of social life, whatever its particular form. All this implies constraints upon human freedom to imagine and make society. Religion sets criteria for judging what human beings do with their social life. It insists that not everything human beings imagine or make is good and worthwhile. It questions whether we are right to regard as valueless everything we have not made ourselves.

That last sentence echoes the comment of Schumacher on the modern economic order. In criticizing the modern tendency to dissipate unrenewable natural resources and to treat irreplaceable capital as though it were income, Schumacher writes: '[W]e are estranged from reality and inclined to treat as valueless everything that we have not made ourselves'.[2] His comment illustrates that viewing society as an artifact might be troublesome not only to the religious, but to any perspective that holds society to be more than the sum of its current members.

The Unger thesis, if unqualified, overlooks the ambiguity of modernity. The critique of modernity has been an increasing preoccupation of philosophers and social theorists, especially since the rise of critical theory and the work of the neo-Marxist Frankfurt School. Reason, once hailed as an instrument of liberation, has become (it is argued) a means of entrapping us in an iron cage of unfreedom, pushing us towards a totally administered, bureaucratized society. The theoretical critique of modernity has become linked with a variety of causes promoted by social activists. There is profound dissatisfaction, both theoretical and practical, with the modern project and its presuppositions. A consistent argument that society is an artifact must come to terms with the reaction against modernity on the Right (which seeks a return to authority and tradition), and on the Left (which seeks anarchism and quietism).

To contend that society is an artifact would seem to betray an uncritical acceptance of modernity. To call society an 'artifact' is to view the formation of society as a *poiesis* (a making) demanding *techne* (a skill), rather than as a *praxis* requiring *arete* (virtue) as well as skill. Such a view adopts one of the presuppositions of modernity – that all human action can be described as a series of techniques, which can be judged by an instrumental rationality in terms of usefulness or success. Human action understood in that way results in a product, but that product may not have been freely chosen by the maker and it may not remain under the maker's control. It may be used for ends the maker does not want or approve.

In contrast, the view that human action is *praxis* emphasizes

[2] E. F. Schumacher, *Small is Beautiful: Economics as if People Mattered* (New York: Harper and Row, 1973), p. 15.

doing, not making. The doing is intrinsically formed by ends freely chosen by the agent. What results may be virtuous or vicious conduct, with morally good or morally evil consequences for social interaction and the cumulative social situation. As individuals choose and follow norms, they are engaged in a process of communication with others that leads to agreements about the institutionalization of norms in the social order.

We can agree that society is the result of free human action. It is not a structure given from above by a superhuman power nor determined from below by natural necessity. The key issue is how we conceive that human agency in the formation of society. Is it as a *making*, requiring only technical skill and to be judged in terms of efficiency or success? Or is it a matter of *doing* (and hence ultimately of *being*), to be judged by norms embodied and pursued in the conduct that intrinsically constitutes social relationships?

These are the principal difficulties I perceive between religion and the Unger thesis – even assuming a fundamental agreement with and sympathy for the thrust of Unger's work. In the remainder of this essay, I will try to explain how, despite a critical attitude towards modernity and an acceptance of the permanent validity of religious faith, I still see society as a conditional result of human freedom.

What is modernity? There have been a variety of answers to that question, though the answers converge in a way that suggests an underlying unity of conception.

Some identify modernity with autonomous self-consciousness. According to this conception, those who are modern have appropriated their own inner freedom, so that they are fundamentally independent of truth-claims, traditions, laws, or norms that cannot be recognized as originating in the inner dynamism of their own consciousness. Modernity's immanence refuses submission to anything that attempts to impose itself upon human consciousness from without in the name of knowledge or of value. Hence for moderns, knowledge must be immanently generated or at least subject to intersubjective verification, not making a purely external claim in the name of tradition or of revelation from on high. As for morality, moderns are self-legislating persons, following moral norms that they themselves have created in a process of reaching agreement with others concerning common needs, interests and values. The project of modernity, not yet completed, is to release human autonomy from constraints that are in fact self-imposed, but have taken on an illusory force of nature-like necessity.

For other thinkers, modernity chiefly implies a contrast with the culture of traditional societies. From this standpoint, the characteristic feature of modernity is differentiation. Traditional cultures are compact. They form undifferentiated totalities. Within them no clear distinction is made among kinds of value or types of meaning. Modern culture is differentiated because it separates value and meaning. In particular, the cognitive is clearly distinguished from the normative and subjective. Although not all knowledge is scientific, that which is cognitive is often defined as that which can be objectively verified as true. In other words, modernity implies the transition from *mythos* to *logos*, because myth mixes together knowledge, norms and subjective expression.

Another understanding of modernity is to see it as a process of rationalization – the gradual rise of reason in history. This was Max Weber's approach. However, Weber had a narrow conception of reason and of rationalization. He identified rationality with *Zweckrationalität*, the instrumental rationality of technique and calculation, of organization and administration. For Weber, reason could not determine the norms by which we guide our lives; it could not lead us to higher values. Thus, reason did not, in Weber's view, lead to universal human freedom. Rather, it led to what he called the 'iron cage' of bureaucratic rationality from which there was no escape. This problem can be called 'the pathology of modernity': rationality stifling rather than expanding freedom, combined with a relativism that denies any rational foundation for moral and spiritual norms and values. Is this the fruit of reason?

Jürgen Habermas argues that the pathology of modernity is not due to rationalization as such, but to the one-sided way in

: thus far developed.[3] There has been a failure to
ocial institutions all the different dimensions of
ermas distinguishes two different types of action:
ational action and communicative action. Each
type of action requires a distinct process of rationalization.
Weber's rationalization (the growth of *Zweckrationalität*) corresponds with purposive–rational actions. The rationalization of
communicative action – neglected by Weber – is radically
different. It means overcoming the forces that systematically
distort human communication, hinder social interaction, and
produce structures of domination.

Of course, Habermas's critique of Weber and the alternative
interpretation of rationality he offers do not alter the fact that
modern society is increasingly dominated by instrumental,
calculative, bureaucratic rationality. It is not therefore surprising that some thinkers see a profound incompatibility between
modernity and religion. Robert Bellah, the sociologist and
religionist, is one of those who find an incompatibility between
modernity and religion. Following Schumacher, he believes
that the ideology of the modern West is subsumed under four
general concepts: positivism, relativism, reductionism and
evolution.[4] Clearly, if modernity is correctly defined by those
'isms', it is indeed incompatible with religion. But it is possible
to show that each of those concepts mirrors only a distorted
facet of modernity, which, when seen more clearly, is free from
the pathology of modernity and compatible with religion.

Positivism, as normally understood, is the view that valid
knowledge must be derived from scientific methods. Adherence
to this view has produced disastrous consequences. It has led
many to deny that human value judgements can have any
objectivity, thus implying that our choices of values are purely
arbitrary decisions based on subjective emotions. It wrongly

3 This is the thesis of his major, two-volume work, *Theorie des kommunikativen Handelns*
   (Frankfurt am Main: Suhrkamp Verlag, 1981), trans. Thomas McCarthy as *The
   Theory of Communicative Action*, 2 vols (Boston: Beacon Press, 1984–7).
4 Robert Bellah, 'Faith communities challenge – and are challenged by – the
   changing world order', in J. Gremillion and W. Ryan, eds., *World Faiths and the New
   World Order: A Muslim–Jewish–Christian Search Begins* (Sponsored by The Inter-
   religious Peace Colloquium, Lisbon, 7–11 November 1977), pp. 148–68.

excludes the form of knowledge found in the historical–hermeneutic disciplines, where access to the object studied could be
attained only through the understanding of meaning (that is,
these disciplines can only derive knowledge from the interpretation of texts, taking into account the context and prior
judgements of both the authors and the interpreter himself).
Positivism has also excluded from knowledge the type of critical
reflection that uncovers hidden forms of domination and
repression (a potent emancipating knowledge).

However, despite the one-sidedness of positivism, it contains
an important insight that, in undistorted form, is compatible
with a more benign view of modernity. That insight is the
differentiation that has marked off the cognitive realm of
meaning from the normative and the expressive cultural
realms. Cognition or knowledge is the discovery of what can be
verified objectively. It differs from the normative, which consists of meanings not discovered but created by human beings.
However, norms are not created out of nothing. They are
formed out of the needs, interests and wants of actual human
beings. The normative thus presupposes and builds upon the
factual truths about human beings established in the cognitive
sphere of culture; but the normative should be distinguished
from the cognitive. Human beings come together in society,
creating norms and embodying them in institutions through a
process of social interaction.

Unger rejects positivist social science on grounds of its
narrowness. It limits itself to seeking narrowly framed explana-
tions for narrowly described phenomena, and gives up the
search for comprehensive social or historical laws. That critique
may be well founded. Nevertheless, as soon as one clearly
distinguishes the cognitive from the normative and expressive,
one has to recognize that human knowledge is limited and
fragmentary, changing and relative. Comprehensive explana-
tions remain largely hypothetical.[5] Positivism, though admittedly in a distorted and exaggerated way, has rightly insisted

5   See Unger's account of the difference between super-theory and ultra-theory, *Social
    Theory: Its Situation and its Task. A Critical Introduction to Politics: A Work in Constructive
    Social Theory* (Cambridge: Cambridge University Press, 1987), pp. 165–9.

that knowledge requires the strict observance of criteria to be valid, and thus must be clearly distinguished from the free creation of norms and the expression of subjective attitudes and feelings.

This qualified acceptance of positivism has inescapable application to religion. Religion, as embodied in religious traditions and in the practices of religious communities, includes a large measure of normative expression and does not always claim absolute truth. Religious beliefs that are authoritatively asserted as dogmas are primarily community rules and only indirectly make propositional truth-claims. However, in so far as they do claim to embody valid knowledge, religious beliefs are subject to the relativity, mutability and cultural limitations of all human knowledge. A large part of the struggle between religion and modernity has stemmed from the reluctance of organized religion to recognize this fact. Overcoming the distortions of positivism should allow the religious to acknowledge the measure of truth in the resistance of positivists to religion's claim to a higher knowledge. It should also allow human creativity to imagine and make society free of the false necessity imposed upon social institutions and practices by religion's excessive claims to higher knowledge.

The second of Bellah's 'isms' is *relativism*. Relativism views reason as a tool for self-preservation and self-interest. Reason is merely a technical instrument for ordering the basically irrational components of human life into systems of manipulation and control. Such systems necessarily have only a relative truth, determined by their usefulness in dominating a particular situation. The diversity of situations gives rise to a diversity of formal systems for their control, each relatively true.

Here again I want to distinguish the valid insight from its distortion. Pluralism captures the positive elements of relativism. The liberal opts for pluralism. Conservatives tend to oppose pluralism. They insist that there is only one valid account of reality. Truth for them is absolute and exclusive, and they denounce liberals as relativists. It is true that liberals have often made only unsatisfactory attempts to conceive and express the goal of pluralism. Pluralism may very easily slip over into relativism. But in a deeper sense, pluralism goes back to a different concept of reason. Reason is understood as an unrestricted openness to reality. Reason is not a mere instrument of calculation, but a way of participating in reality, and ultimately in the Infinite, the Transcendent. But reason remains finite, a limited participation in the Unlimited. Pluralism in this context is the response of finite intelligence to a reality so rich that it constantly escapes existing categories and calls for the convergence and complementarity of various cultures and modes of experience. Pluralism is the counterpart of finitude. Where pluralism is denied, finitude is forgotten, and faith is corrupted into an idolatrous absolutizing of one of its particular expressions.

From the standpoint of religion, the insistence upon society as an artifact and the rejection an alleged necessity that would exclude our freedom to remake the institutional order of society is the overcoming of idolatry and superstition. At the same time, one can only regret the use of the concept of 'artifact', which is redolent of a calculative or purely formal rationality.

Our third 'ism' is *reductionism*, which is defined by Bellah as the belief that all higher manifestations of life are nothing but disguised expressions of class intersts, libidinal energies or other lower determinants. Reductionism in that pejorative sense makes of analysis a sort of pathology. Unger's work is the very opposite of reductionistic, because his analysis (particularly his distinction between routine and framework) specifically seeks to counter lower-level determinants and to release human imagination and freedom in the transformation of society. We are not completely governed by the established imaginative and institutional contexts of our societies, says Unger; nor are these contexts entirely determined by general laws (hence Unger's rejection of the deep-structure social theory of Marx). Unger's analysis will tend to quiet religious fears of reductionism. But is the religious claim that man is not the highest authority compatible with such a radical interpretation of social freedom?

Bellah's fourth and last constituent of modern ideology is *evolution*. But evolution, as applied to social phenomena and history, can be interpreted in two fundamentally different ways. Bellah and Schumacher view evolution as a natural and automatic process, determined by such biological factors as competition and the survival of the fittest. This implicitly denies the human ability to revise not only the routine, but also the context of human action. It is incompatible with the anti-naturalistic social theory of Unger. It is also incompatible with religious hope.

But there is a second way of understanding social evolution, which is to see it as the effect of human rationality in history. Reason follows an orderly (or 'logical' in the wider sense of that term) sequence in the answering of questions and the solution of problems. The answering of one question opens up a new question; the solving of one problem makes it possible to discern the solution to another related problem. There is nothing automatic about the process. People can ignore, forget or suppress answers to age-old problems. There can be regress as well as progress in human history. Nevertheless, in so far as rationality governs human action, there is a development or evolution in human knowledge and practice. The evolution is more marked in the sphere of science and technique where moral values are not directly a factor. But even in the sphere of ethics, some development is discernible.

The modern ideology of evolution has a complex relationship to traditional religious belief. It reinforces the Western religious view that history is linear, but clashes with the Eastern conception of cyclical history. It shares with religion a hope in eventual human perfection, but secularizes that hope, denying its transcendent sources. In its secular form, it often swings from hope to despair, producing dystopias as well as utopias.

Is, then, modernity compatible or incompatible with religion? The answer is bound to be qualified. Modernity designates a fundamental shift in human culture, which can be roughly circumscribed with key words – freedom, science, rationalization, differentiation. In contrast, traditional culture is tied to such words as authority, perennial truth, reason, compactness. That shift, I contend, has taken place in a one-sided fashion, producing distortion. In their distorted form, represented by positivism, relativism, and a purely calculative rationality, the insights of modernity are incompatible with religious faith. In their authentic form they are not, though their acceptance demands a transformation in the conventional understanding of religion. I now examine that transformation in its relation to the making and the reform of society.

Upon what does the social and political life of human beings rest? What is the foundation of human society? There are undeniably pre-rational factors: blood-relationship; a particular natural environment; the pressure of basic needs for food, shelter and protection; the continuance of common interests. However, if we are to distinguish human society from the horde, we must acknowledge the intervention of human rational intelligence in articulating common needs and interests, and in further developing and institutionalizing the manifold instances of social interaction. Society thus becomes a project of human intelligence, a work of human reason. We can therefore ask: what is the scope of human creativity in the making of society? What is the rational foundation, the foundation within human reason, upon which society is built?

Society as the product and expression of human rationality cannot rest upon the empirical sciences, which produce not ultimate truths, but only probable findings. Those sciences deal with facts, not values or norms. Admittedly, fact and value are inextricably intertwined in the social sciences, so that non-trivial judgements of fact always presuppose some prior judgements of value. None the less, scientific methodology is not appropriate for answering questions of value. As noted above, positivists give a purely decisionist or emotivist account of values, denying them any rational foundation. But society as a human, rational enterprise cannot be built upon empirically determined fact alone. The moral norms so essential to society are less concerned with what human beings are than with what they ought to be. To try to draw norms from empirical fact alone is to identify success, however achieved, with moral goodness. Such an approach canonizes the existing order because there is no basis from which to criticize it. It hands society over to the technocrat, and makes the process of efficient goal-attainment supreme over the public discussion of the goals and values themselves. We have witnessed this process in our own time – an unquestioning devotion to the process of continuous economic expansion – and have seen how it can have disastrous consequences and, indeed, can call the entire project of modernity into question.

For the building of society, we must therefore appeal to a higher order of truth than mere empirical fact. We must ask fundamental questions: what is the human condition? What is the order of the values governing human action? What is the nature of human relationships? What may human beings reasonably expect? Such questions can be tackled only through religious and philosophical argument. Kant summed up his work as a critical philosopher in three questions: what can we know? What ought we to do? What can we hope for? The answer we give to each of these questions will profoundly affect the manner in which we endeavour to transform society. Even so, does that mean a turning back to the dominance of politics by metaphysical or theological systems, and the imposition of a pre-written script upon social and political experience? If we organize society in the light of unchanging truths, shall we not give to social institutions a supremacy they should not have?

Certainly, that was the pre-modern, traditional approach, reinforced by an appeal to religious truth as found in divine revelation. The social order was seen as part of the cosmic order, created by God. Although the fall of humanity and the resultant sinfulness affected the social order, established institutions generally enjoyed divine providence. Such varied theologians as Augustine, Martin Luther, Robert Bellarmine and Leo XIII have taught that divine providence sanctions human rulership, so that political authority is invested with sacredness. Though exceptions to the duty of submission have always been allowed (often reluctantly), the usual attitude inculcated through Christianity has been unquestioning obedience to the ruling powers. Behind such an attitude lay the conviction that life in society rested upon universal truths about the human condition, human nature and human sinfulness. Although rebellion might at times be helpful in rescuing society from a tyrant, no radical remaking of society should follow. Further-more, the universal truths suggested that only one type of social organization was ideally suited to the human condition.

The modern acceptance of pluralism – in particular, ideo-logical pluralism – and the individual freedom that follows from pluralism has changed all that. How can a society be founded upon pluralism? I find the answer to this question in a statement of Thomas Gilby: 'Civilization is formed of men [and women] locked together in argument. From this dialogue the community becomes a political community.'[6] This process of rational deliberative argument within political associations, John Courtney Murray has commented, is a unique feature of human society.[7]

What is the argument about? According to Murray, it has three major themes: public affairs (matters requiring public decision and action by government); affairs of the common-wealth (matters outside the scope of government but bearing upon the quality of common life, such as education); and the constitutional consensus (matters that give a society its identity and sense of purpose). As Murray notes, the argument does not cease when agreement is reached. On the contrary, argument presupposes a context of agreement. This is so with scientific and philosophical argument, and it is likewise true of political argument. If there is a civilized society, there will be a context of agreement, from which argument can proceed. What is the content of the social agreement? Murray, whose general stance is conservative, sees the agreement as a patrimony of substan-tive truths, a heritage of rational belief, a structure of basic knowledge. While there is thus an ensemble of agreed affirma-tions, argument continues because the content of the consensus must be constantly scrutinized and developed in light of ongoing political experience.

We may grant Murray that every civilized society has a patrimony of agreed truths and values that serve as the initial

6 Thomas Gilby, *Between Community and Society: A Philosophy and Theology of the State* (New York: Longmans/Green, 1953), p. 93.
7 John Courtney Murray, *We Hold These Truths: Catholic Reflections on the American Proposition* (New York: Sheed and Ward, 1960), pp. 5–24.

context and starting point of argument. But given the present struggle between liberal pluralists and fundamentalists, between those who welcome and advocate radical changes in our traditional beliefs and those who staunchly insist upon the total validity of established tradition, we should not overstate the extent of our common social ground. Rather, we must identify the minimum level of consensus required to base society on rational argument. I suggest that, at a minimum, we must agree to those truths and values implicit in the acceptance of rational argument as the appropriate basis for political society.

This suggestion directly links the generally conservative Murray to the neo-Marxist Habermas. In his communicative theory of society, Habermas distinguishes two types of human action: purposive–rational action and communicative action.[8] Purposive–rational action is directed at success – that is, the efficient achievement of ends by appropriate means. Communicative action is directed to mutual understanding, leading to an agreement. Communicative action, as suggested earlier, is essential for an emancipated society. Purposive–rational action alone leads to the 'iron cage' of bureaucratic rationality.

All communicative action takes place in the context of consensus, but that consensus may break down. Since consensus requires acceptance of the validity-claims raised in communicative action, the consensus breaks down when these validity-claims are questioned or rejected by the participants. Consensus must then be restored, Habermas suggests, by moving to the 'level of discourse' – that is, to argumentation. Discourse or argumentation is governed by what Habermas calls the 'ideal speech situation', an ideal-type or counter-factual hypothesis of a situation where the only force is the force of the better argument, with all other types of coercion or domination being excluded. The ideal speech situation provides both a model and a rational foundation for an emancipated society. It provides a model, because it embodies the essential values of such a society: freedom, equality and justice.

[8]   Habermas, *Communication and the Evolution of Society* (Boston: Beacon Press, 1979).

It provides a rational foundation, because these values are implied in the ideal speech situation. Thus, for Habermas as well as Murray, a civilized or emancipated society is an association built upon the permanence of rational argumentation, based on a consensus about the truths and values necessarily implied in rational argumentation itself.

In this conception of a pluralistic society, built upon consensus rather than obedience, what is the function of religion? Here I must distinguish my views from Habermas, for whom religion is obsolete, and from Murray, for whom religion is an orthodoxy, and give my own interpretation of the role of religion in modern society.

It is first necessary to distinguish faith and beliefs. Faith is the fundamental religious response. It is an orientation towards the Transcendent, an unrestricted opening of the mind and heart to Reality as Unlimited, or to the Infinite. It can be described as a basic trust in Reality or as a universal love of Reality. It is not merely relatively transcendent, but absolutely so, inasmuch as it is a thrust beyond every human order of meaning, beyond all the particular forms through which it is mediated in the different religious traditions. As an orientation it has a term, 'the Transcendent', but no object, because the Transcendent remains unknown. The term of the response of faith is mystery, because we have no proper knowledge of the Transcendent. We cannot grasp the Transcendent as an object; we can merely indicate the Infinite, the Unlimited, through symbols.

The response of religious faith as an awareness of the Transcendent constitutes a fundamental stance of the subject which, like an originating idea, takes possession of the mind and heart and widens the horizon within which the person thinks, judges, decides and acts. This, in turn, gives rise to a body of religious beliefs. The fundamental stance or originating idea provokes and governs the apprehension and judgement of values. Judgements of value constitute the first type of religious belief. The second type is judgements of fact. Factual beliefs arise as the mind, animated by faith, strives to interpret a profusion of data about the external world and the interior world of consciousness. Both kinds of religious belief – judgements of value and judgements of fact – are thus the product of interpretative reflection by the human mind within the horizon opened up by faith. The function of religious beliefs in shaping society is to form part of the patrimony of truths and values that are debated through politics. Societies begin not with a *tabula rasa*, but with an inherited tradition; religious beliefs are always part of that tradition. Like all human creations, however, religious beliefs are relative, mutable and limited by culture. To suppose otherwise is to fall into idolatry, making the conditional unconditioned and confusing religious beliefs with religious faith. Religious beliefs are the changing, limited, culturally particular manifestation of religious faith. Therefore, in political argument, religious people must be prepared to see their religious beliefs challenged. They must refrain from using any weapons to advance their beliefs other than the force of the better argument. To act otherwise is to substitute the political argument of civilized society for the brute force of barbarism. The religious, and religious institutions, can only help to complete the project of modernity (that is, releasing the social enterprise from all false necessity) if they advance their beliefs as something other than unchanging and unquestionable. Those beliefs can then enter fruitfully into the political argument.

Does religious faith have a role in this process that is distinct from the role of particular beliefs? Yes; it has the vital role of keeping the argument open. Religious faith may be seen as following a narrow ridge between the two abysses of nihilism and idolatry. Nihilism denies the validity of all truths and values and reduces human life and human society to a contest of unrestrained selfishness and exploitation. Idolatry, in contrast, makes one set of truths and values absolute and seeks to freeze human life and society into conformity with those beliefs. Both nihilism and idolatry refuse the authority of rational political argument; both remain content with a purely calculative rationality. It is a mistake to suppose that human beings easily relinquish their prejudices or readily allow their cherished convictions to be questioned. Political arguments that touch deep-seated truths and values cannot be sustained unless the members of society can transcend their individual selves (and, indeed, transcend humanity itself) to open out to Unlimited Reality with an unlimited response. Religious faith is best viewed not as a set of beliefs, but as an unrestricted openness to Reality. As such, it is a critical foundation for the permanent argument that constitutes political society. Human rationality, when taken beyond the efficient adaptation of means to ends, is a more fragile and elusive achievement than we often realize. Paradoxically, it requires religious faith for its survival.

Religion has historically played both socially integrative and revolutionary roles in society. Both religious belief and religious faith have contributed to each role. First, consider the role of religious beliefs. Some beliefs support submission to the existing institutions of society and strengthen the established order; for example, the belief in God as author of the cosmic and social order. Other beliefs, such as the teaching of the Hebrew prophets on social justice or the Gospel message of concern for the poor and the outcast, are revolutionary in their implications. Within the same religious tradition are specific teachings that can be selected to support opposing views. This does not mean that religious beliefs are simply used to bolster pre-existing prejudices. The possibility of diverse interpretation simply shows the need for argument.

The role of religious faith in society is primarily a revolutionary one (though perhaps I should say 'transforming' to avoid some of the intellectual baggage that comes with the word 'revolutionary'). Religious faith, by pushing us towards the Transcendent, relativizes every existing order. In so far as any existing social order absolutizes itself, religious faith becomes subversive and revolutionary in the usual political sense. The difference between revolution and other kinds of social change is that revolution calls into question the principles of rulership and the legitimacy of the existing social order. Since every social order tends to make itself absolute, it is the constant function of religious faith to remind human beings that even basic principles are subject to revision as human understanding grows. Religious faith protects human creativity from social inertia.

There are two reasons, however, why it is misleading to speak of religious faith as revolutionary in the ordinary, political sense. Revolutionary movements and ideologies often yield to the temptation to absolutize themselves and their cause. But religious faith rejects all absolutism – both that of the existing order and that of particular revolutions. Authentic religious faith resists the fanaticism of both Right and Left, of both revolutionary millenarianism and the ideology of Christendom. There is a utopian element in religious faith (for example, unfailing hope), but unrestricted utopianism is a corruption of faith, forgetting as it does that the term of religious faith is mystery, not a product of human desire.

The second reason why religious faith is not necessarily revolutionary is that 'revolution' stresses the overthrow of the old rather than the emergence of the new. But religion is primarily concerned with transformation and only secondarily with destruction. The old is renewed, not annihilated. Even when religion speaks of apocalypse, it is far more concerned with the coming of the new order (for example, the new Jerusalem) than with the destruction of the old.

If some have found these reflections too wide ranging, I can only plead that they attempt to respond to a very wide-ranging book. I hope, however, that the central thrust of my reply to Unger is clear. He has set out to develop the idea of society as artifact to the hilt. As a religious thinker I find myself in agreement with that aim, in part because it provides a better framework for defining the relation of religion to society than other social theories. But I have one major proviso: Unger's project should be cleansed of a narrow conception of reason (as merely a calculative instrument or tool for efficient manipulation), and should embrace the wider conception articulated by Habermas (which includes reason as a means to communicative action). The narrower conception of reason is unfortunately reflected in the programmatic sentence: 'Society is an artifact'. I am calling attention to the need to free the project of modernity from the pathology of modernity.

CHAPTER 2

The present social function of religion

The question of what has happened to religion with the emergence of the modern world is a difficult one to answer.[1] The last chapter focused on one particular feature of modernity, namely, the recognition that society is a human construct, the product of human agency. The problem of religion and modernity is wider than that. There is disagreement both about the features that constitute modern society as distinctively modern and about the defining characteristics of religion. If we do not agree on what modernity means and on what religion means, how can we relate the two?

Until the 1960s religious people, especially Catholics, saw the modern world as essentially hostile to Christian faith and life. John XXIII was the first pope to stop deploring the modern world and, instead, to speak positively of its achievements. The common Christian view was that the modern world in its beginnings in the Enlightenment and the French Revolution was built on a rejection of both the truth of the Christian faith and the authority of the Christian churches. Modernity meant secularism, which in turn meant the exclusion of religion from the public life and decision-making process of society. No wonder the modern world and Christianity were in opposition.

Then in the sixties came a dramatic change of attitude. In his best-seller *The Secular City* (London: SCM Press, 1965), Harvey

---

[1] My reflections on this theme were stimulated by attending a conference, *Christianisme et Modernité*, at the Centre Justice et Foi, Montreal, in August 1987. It was there that I first learned of Gauchet's book, on which this chapter is largely based. The lack of attention to it in the English-speaking world shows that communication even in Quebec is not an easy achievement.

Cox wrote with enthusiasm of secular values and secular society, regarding the acknowledgement of their integrity and relative autonomy as bound up with Christian faith in the Creation and Incarnation. Secularity – respecting the secular world with its tasks and values – should not, he said, be confused with anti-religious secularism. Although Harvey Cox was himself a Baptist, his book had a notable impact upon Catholics. Vatican II also encouraged Catholics to turn towards the modern world with its tasks and values, particularly those related to social justice.

The enthusiasm of the sixties did not last. A period of disillusionment, if not despair, followed. The secular city did not look so wonderful after Vietnam, the nuclear arms race, and the increase in poverty and unemployment. Many felt they were living in a society without compassion, run by cynics.

Further, some people began to question the presuppositions of the so-called theology of secularization. This theology assumed that the dynamic of the Christian faith is towards the secularization of society and culture, and so towards the decline of religion in the traditional sense in which it provided the overall context for all our affairs, even worldly ones, penetrating them with its language, claims and values. Dietrich Bonhoeffer was a young German theologian who denounced Hitler from the beginning of Nazism. At the outbreak of World War II he returned to Germany from the USA, where he had been on a lecture tour, and worked for the overthrow of Hitler. He was arrested in April 1943 and hanged two years later. During his imprisonment he reflected on the present state of Christianity. He expressed his thought in letters and papers which were smuggled out of the prison; they were published under the title *Letters and Papers from Prison* (London and Glasgow: Collins Fontana Books, 1959). Their publication released a vigorous controversy, especially over his idea that Christianity should now cast off the religious framework in which up till now it has been understood and presented. Hence the catchword 'religionless Christianity'. But the proliferation of religious movements and new religious cults led some people, including sociologists, to a very different conclusion. They vehemently denied that religion was declining and argued that we were witnessing a return to religion. Christians, they urged, should be relating their faith to these widespread religious aspirations, not chasing after the failed modern project of building a secular society without religion.

The theological debate about secularization is linked to the political debate over neo-conservatism and the shift to the Right and to the cultural debate on the transition from modernity to post-modernity. Post-modernity has been interpreted and evaluated in two opposing ways: as the continuation and completion of the modern project on the one hand, and as anti-modernity on the other.

In 1986, a book appeared in France which confounds our expectations and alters the direction of the debate: *Le Désenchantement du monde: Une histoire politique de la religion* (Paris: Gallimard, 1986) by Marcel Gauchet. In many respects it is a revival of the secularization thesis, recently in disfavour, which sees secular society as the end result of Christianity itself. But its analysis runs much deeper than was previously the case and, in particular, Gauchet upsets our usual conception of religion and its history. He describes Christianity as 'la religion de la sortie de la religion' (the religion that brings about the exit from religion), and declares that the history of the Christian religion came to an end around 1700. In general terms, the trajectory of religion in our world, the modern world, is now over.

However, he does not make this judgement from an antireligious standpoint (one that envisions human beings as finally freeing themselves from the incubus of religion). As his subtitle indicates, Gauchet is concerned with the political history of religion. He traces the functioning of religion as a structural principle of society through its metamorphoses in history to the paradoxical outcome that men and women are led to reconstruct human society outside of religion and, indeed, contrary to the logic of religion.

Further, as Gauchet himself insists, the end of religion of which he speaks is the social end of religion. In this view, religion has become outdated as a structural principle of society, but that does not exclude the continuance, even the perpetuity, of other forms of religious experience on the level of thought, imagination and self-consciousness. Religion as structure has come to an end because its function has been reabsorbed in the worldly human; religion as a culture, however, still remains. Religious faith is subjectively anchored in a manner that Gauchet neither denies nor analyses. His focus, as I have said, is upon the political function and history of religion.

Gauchet's unusual account of religio-political history is based on a particular understanding of religion. He conceives of religion as the way of thinking and acting which presupposes that society with its structure is given prior to human agency and is therefore unchangeable. The social order is not established and articulated by human beings but has its source elsewhere. Hence religion is identified as a social system that dispossesses the members of society of their political power. They can repeat the old, but they cannot create the new. In other words, all that human beings can and should do is accept the order of things as a sacred legacy to be preserved unchanged and handed on to the next generation.

The idea that the social order has its source outside of human agency and is thus already given as immutable prior to human activity is found in its purest form in primitive societies – societies at the stage of development prior to the emergence of the State. At that stage of development, the founding of the social order is attributed to gods and heroes who live in mythical time, the time before historical time, the primordial time of the beginnings, including the beginnings of social institutions. They and their founding of the social order belong to the primordial past, while we live in the present, and such a difference of times is unbridgeable. What separation could be greater than a temporal one, with the past time of the beginnings of a different order from the present time? In contrast, when the high god of monotheism became, as Creator, the founder of the social order, the separation was conceived spatially, with him in heaven and us on earth. But the separation involved in such a spatial distancing was not absolute. Hence it became possible to claim communication with the Creator and to introduce modifications under the cover of interpreting his decrees. The systematic blocking by religion of innovation and change was thus weakened.

The conclusion follows – and Gauchet does not flinch from it, but makes it a major theme of his book – that religion was at its high point, its purest form and most effective functioning, at the beginning. We have to invert our perspective. We usually take the rise of the great religions as an advance and purification of religious consciousness. But Gauchet regards what we interpret as the development of religion as being instead its decline – a weakening of its function. From its point of greatest power over human society at the beginning, the religious system has undergone a series of transformations that has finally put it outside the structure of society.

There have been three major transformations of the religious system. The first was linked to the emergence of the State. The second was marked by the concept of a transcendent God and the religious attitude of renunciation of the world. The third was the Christian transformation, in which the political function of religion came to an end.

Gauchet lays great stress on the coming of the State and the transformation it brought. Before the State, in the period when the religious system was in its purest form, there was no political power in the full sense. The tribal chief could not introduce anything. He had simply to ensure the continuation of what had always been done and see to the unfailing repetition of the myth. The source or principle of order was outside the human world. With the State, that principle came into the human world through the establishment of ruling élites, who exercise power over society in the name of God. It was a first step in the reabsorption of the power of the founders of society, which would lead eventually to the assumption of that power by all in a system of equality. The power of some in the name of God was the beginning of the power of all in regard to the laws and decrees claiming to come from God. With the emergence of the State, human agency asserted its claim against the priority and immutability of the religious system.

The second transformation was a feature of what the philosopher Karl Jaspers called the axial period of human history (from 800 to 200 BC). It was the emergence of a new spiritual consciousness linked to an attitude of renunciation of this world. The 'renouncers' gained a new independence from the State and the political order. During the first period after the emergence of the State, the political order was dominant over the religious system. Now, with the new inwardness, there was a degree of separation of religion from the political order.

It is thus possible to see religion in terms of the division and separation it brought. In the first instance, religion established a separation between the human world and its exterior source of order. Then in the next stage, with the emergence of the State, there was a division between the rulers and the people, the rulers representing the religious source of order. With the belief in a transcendent God and the attitude of renouncing the world, the division brought by religion became an interior one. The religious imperative was to be detached from this world in order to enter into harmony with a higher or transcendent order of reality. God as the source of order was drawn into the human world, but in becoming less remote – less exterior – he became an interior reality, located in consciousness.

The conclusion Gauchet draws from that analysis contradicts the contention going back to the nineteenth-century philosopher Ludwig Feuerbach that what is given to the gods is taken away from human beings. According to that contention, the greater the gods, the more diminished are human beings. The greater the gods, declares Gauchet, the freer are human beings because the hold of divine law and the degree of obligation it creates are lessened in proportion to the concentration and separation of the divine in a unified and transcendent God. The more distant the transcendent Deity, the more divine laws and decrees call for interpretation, mediation and varied application. Hence the increased function of human agency and the greater possibility of change. The power of religion to determine human life is thus weakened.

The third, or Christian, transformation led to the cessation of religion as a structural principle of society. What happened from the Middle Ages onwards was not a process of laicization, as if a new set of profane values gradually took over from existing sacred values. Instead, there took place a sacred legitimation of the secular realm, which changed being-for-the-other-world into being-in-this-world.

In its conflict with the Church, the temporal power's position was based on the ideas of the sacredness of the Ruler coming directly from God and the duty to appropriate this world as God's creation. As a result, the argument ran, the Church could not claim to be the sole authorized mediator. Pope Gelasius in his famous statement of 494 tried to reconcile spiritual and temporal power through a double mutual subordination. The world, declared Gelasius, is governed by two powers: the sacred authority of the Pontiff and the royal power. The Pontiff is superior in higher, spiritual affairs, but inferior in lower, temporal matters. Clearly such a relationship was unworkable. Not surprisingly, the popes were led to arrogate to themselves all power in the name of the higher things in their charge. The counterclaim of the secular rulers that they were directly authorized by God in governing the affairs of this world led in the event to secular society.

The Christian order was essentially unstable in its attempts to find a compromise between acceptance and rejection of this world. Christians were called upon to live in this world but not to be of this world – in other words, to keep themselves outside the world in which they must live. This compromise was a reflection of the doctrine of the conjunction of the two natures in Christ, each nature remaining intact.

At this point the analysis of Gauchet joins Louis Dumont's widely remarked account of the origin of Christian individualism.[2] A form of individualism arose in India and elsewhere among the 'renouncers of this world'. The religious attitude of renunciation *vis-à-vis* the world freed ascetics from the collectivity, so that the individual as such emerged in history. In its beginnings the Christian religion adopted the same renunciation. Hence the Christian individual was at first otherworldly, constituted as an individual in relation to God. But Christia-

---

[2] Louis Dumont, *Essays on Individualism: Modern Ideology in Anthropological Perspective* (Chicago: University of Chicago Press, 1986).

nity achieved what no Indian religion fully attained, a fellow-
ship of love in a community of equals. Through its teaching on
the essential equality of all and the strength of the link with this
world because of the doctrine of the Incarnation, the other-
worldly individual of early Christianity was transformed into
the innerworldly individual of modern society.

Such, then, is Gauchet's account of the political history of
religion. His book is a difficult one to read, as French reviewers
have confessed. I have sketched his analysis with broad strokes
that hardly do justice to the profundity and detail of his
thought. Nevertheless, enough has been said to raise again the
question with which I began: what has happened to religion
with the emergence of the modern world?

The traditional social form of religion, which presupposed
that religion was a structuring principle of society, is now
obsolete. The social end of religion is in that sense a fact. We
live irretrievably in a secular society. Once it has been grasped
that the social order is a result of human agency, not a pattern
imposed by some exterior or transcendent principle, there can
be no going back from that insight. Religion can no longer be,
as it was in the past, the ground of the social and political order.
Christians should resist the nostalgia for Christendom, that is,
for a society and culture based upon a unity in the Christian
faith. Gauchet has provided us with a profound analysis of the
process and end result of the gradual dissolution of religion as a
social system.

However, that is not the whole story. The continuance of
religion as the experience of the Unlimited Order that lies as
the unknown term at the end of human striving has a social
impact, now that social existence has taken a subjective form,
in which everything comes under the will of the human agents
constituting the membership of the society and is the fruit of
their collective will. Religion, while no longer a structural
principle, can still be a social factor. It can relate to society as a
critical principle. Its exclusion from the institutional structure
has released it as a permanent critique.

This suggests a new understanding of power and empowerment when applied to the social action of religious people.

Since religion is not part of the structure of modern society, it cannot legitimately use violence or coercion to promote its policy and values. Its social action must find expression in non-violent forms. But this break with violence by religion has a positive side. It suggests that the present witness of religious people should be the teaching and example of non-violence. It would take a separate essay to expound this fully, but in brief, non-violence has come to the fore in recent times as a religious option because the present social function of religion is to bring humankind to that new level of social existence characterized by non-violence. The successive transformations of society may have rendered the traditional social functions of religion obsolete, but a further transformation is now called for: the elimination of violence as a normative social principle. If deprived of its other functions, religion has a role waiting for it there.

CHAPTER 3

From inwardness to social action: the transformation of the political

There is now general agreement that Christians, by virtue of their Christian commitment, should engage in social and political action, particularly on behalf of the poor and oppressed. That is the presupposition behind Liberation Theology. At the same time the conviction persists that social and political action is not properly religious action, but, strictly speaking, only the consequence or overflow of religion into a non-religious, secular sphere. Hence the felt necessity, especially on the part of those with religious authority, to qualify the acceptance of Liberation Theology with frequent warnings that the Christian religion should not be *reduced* to social and political action.[1]

More widespread among ordinary religious people is the manner in which the perennial need for reflection becomes a devaluing of social and political action in favour of interior contemplation as alone truly religious. People are urged to withdraw at regular intervals from their social involvement, which is dubbed external activity, in order to find God once more in the properly religious activity of personal, meditative prayer. The religious life is seen as the inner life in contrast to the outer life. The locus of the Transcendent and of religious experience is identified with the realm of interiority. To work for the liberation of the poor and oppressed may be demanded by religious faith, hope and love. It is applied religion, but it is

---

[1] For the relationship of Political and Liberation Theology to social and political action and the difficult question to which this relationship gives rise, see Chapter 3, 'Faith and social policy' in my book, *Theology and Political Society* (Cambridge: Cambridge University Press, 1980), pp. 51–74.

not of the essence of religion, which is found in the inwardness of union with God.

This tendency of the Christian religion has been strongly reinforced by interest in the Eastern religions. Outside the academic study of those religions, interest has focused upon their contribution to the exploration of states of consciousness and to the development of deep inwardness or concentration. In being exported to the West, the religions of the East have necessarily been stripped of their social and political framework and implications. Hence the conviction among both religious and secular people today that all religion is concerned with the deepening and unification of individual, interior consciousness, whether in the Western form of union with God or the Eastern form of absorption into the One.

I want to argue that this persistent conviction that religion is to be identified with interiority is wrong on two counts. First, it rests upon a faulty understanding of modern culture and, second, its conception of religious experience is mistaken. Inwardness or the withdrawal into the inner depths of consciousness is not a whit more religious than social and political action. Furthermore, it is at least arguable that in our present historical situation if there is any privileged locus for religious experience it is not the interior realm but social interaction.

To take first the question of modern culture. As I briefly indicated in Chapter 1, the phrase 'modern culture' implies a contrast with the culture of traditional societies. An analysis widely held, though given different formulations, sees differentiation of cultural spheres as a characteristic feature of modernity. Traditional cultures are compact. They form undifferentiated totalities. Within them no clear distinction is made among kinds of values or types of meaning. Modern culture is differentiated because it marks off spheres of value or, from another standpoint, realms of meaning. A representative analysis and one helpful here makes a threefold distinction: the cognitive, the normative and the expressive.

The cognitive cultural sphere mediates objective reality, reality as over against the subject as subject, and thus expands

and develops the realm of human knowing. Through knowledge human beings discover surrounding reality as intelligible
and affirm as truth what they discover. Not all knowledge is
scientific, but modern science has led to the clear differentiation
of the cognitive as the sphere of what can be objectively verified
as true.

The second or normative cultural sphere consists of meanings, not discovered, but created by human beings through
social interaction. Human beings all share a set of needs,
interests and wants. These are not just instinctual drives, but
find appropriate expression as ideals and values and thus allow
for a comparative evaluation and ordering. Human beings
come together in society and through a process of social
communication and interaction create a normative order out of
the needs, interests, wants, ideals and values of its members,
both as individuals and in groups. The norms thus created are
embodied in the institutions of society. As institutionalized,
they constitute the various sub-orders of society, such as the
economic order, the political order, the legal order, and that
general order of communication and interaction we sometimes
call the life-world.

Norms are not created out of nothing. They are formed out
of the needs, interests and wants of actual human beings. The
normative sphere, therefore, presupposes and builds upon the
factual truths about human beings established in the cognitive
sphere of culture. All the same, the two spheres should be
differentiated. There is a variety of ideals and values and
conflict among them when related to concrete reality. The
normative order of society is derived from the free choice of
human beings. Cultures differ according to which needs, wants
and interests are made normative and following which scale of
values. There is no single normative order to be discovered. To
suppose so is to confuse the cognitive and the normative
cultural spheres. Human creativity in imagining and establishing possible social orders is not unlimited, but it allows for a
range of possibilities. Conflict of choices should in principle be
resolved through the very process of social communication and
action, with agreement as the aim, if not the achievement.

The third or expressive cultural sphere is that of subject as subject. It is constituted by the exploration, articulation and expression of the reality of the subject. Here what is sought is truthfulness rather than the truth of the first sphere, sincerity rather than the normative practice of the second sphere. Further, the subjective states are explored and expressed for their own sake. They are not examined primarily for any objective cognitive content they might yield. To enter into different states of consciousness, to plunge into depths of the human psyche, is to explore a world, the inward world of the human subject. To articulate what is discovered there is the motivating force behind much poetry and prose. However, not all subjective awareness reaches such heights or depths, and a common, ordinary feature of modern culture is the differentiation of subjective as subjective.

In brief, then, one can say that modern culture distinguishes three worlds, to all of which human beings are related in their living: the external or objective world of human knowledge, the social world of practice with its norms, and the subjective world of self-awareness. Because those three worlds have emerged as distinct, modern culture clearly differentiates the objective from the subjective, history and society from nature, sincerity and truthfulness from objective truth.[2]

I have not marked out a distinct cultural sphere for religious faith and experience. The first mistake of those who identify religion with inwardness is to suppose, in analysing modern culture, that religion should be marked off as constituting a distinct realm of meaning or of practice. To suppose so is in effect to deny that religious reality transcends all human meanings and each and every human world. Transcendence does not form a realm of meaning or cultural world, alongside the other three, but is the Unlimited that lies beyond, while underpinning and penetrating each of the three worlds and any other that human culture should distinguish. Religious faith

---

[2] For Habermas's distinction of three domains of reality and the respective validity-claims that each makes see his essay, 'What is universal pragmatics?', in Jürgen Habermas, *Communication and the Evolution of Society* (Boston: Beacon Press, 1979), pp. 1–68.

arises from a boundary experience, an experience of finitude, which may occur in any of the three human worlds. There is no such thing as human faith pure and simple, but there are, instead, three types or forms of religion, corresponding to the three cultural spheres.

Religious faith is primarily rooted in a negative experience: an experience of the nothingness, the emptiness, the non-meaning into which each of the limited worlds of human meaning plunges at its limits. It is the dynamic tension towards the Unlimited that can survive the disintegration of every human world and underpin the new world that replaces the old, because it recognizes the finitude of every human world. Such faith, going beyond all humanly apprehensible meaning, has no positive content of its own. There are no specifically religious images or concepts. There is no specifically religious language. All religious images and concepts are drawn from one or other of three cultural spheres with their finite content and made to mean the Beyond by a process of extrapolation, intensification, hyperbole or extravagance. Transcendent reality is thus indirectly or symbolically expressed and brought to bear upon human thought and practice. It remains, however, beyond any direct grasp or experience and for that reason has no conceptual or imaginative expression properly its own.

It follows that to suppose – the first mistake – that religion constitutes a distinct world, defined as sacred over against the secular of the three human worlds, entails a second mistake, namely an erroneous conception of religious experience. The error is to claim a direct, literal apprehension of the Transcendent, so as to give positive content to that sacred world, and thus to fall into idolatry by identifying the Transcendent with its finite symbols.

But an error about Transcendence involves an error about Immanence. To make religion a distinct world or cultural sphere is to overlook that the Transcendent is related to every human world or cultural sphere as its animating principle, underpinning its meaning and value, and thus to deny the Immanence of the Transcendent. Although the Transcendent lies beyond every human realm of meaning, and thus is experienced primarily only negatively, as the Unlimited in meaning and value, it stands as the impossible which human beings must consciously reach out for if they are to attain the possible. For that reason, the exclusion of the sacred from the differentiated cultural spheres is proving disastrous for modern culture. It marks a failure to open up these 'secular' spheres to the Beyond in symbols and images, and has resulted in a stultification and trivialization of cultural content, together with a demonic absolutizing of the impoverished meaning and values. The effect upon religion, which has been seduced into trying to maintain itself as a distinct cultural sphere, is to make it canonize obsolete cultural elements as sacred. Because these elements, drawn from the past, are no longer features of contemporary culture, they can be proclaimed as sacred. The social relationships of a bygone age are thus mystified as the sacred structure of Christ's Church.

Am I arguing for an empty Beyond? In one sense, yes. There is no direct apprehension or experience of the Transcendent. Hence those living in the tension towards the Beyond are plunged sooner or later into a void, an emptiness, a nothingness. That inevitably has been articulated most explicitly in the contemplative form of religion, with its dark nights or emptying of consciousness, but it applies to the other forms of religion as well. In another sense, I am arguing not for an empty Beyond, but for the reality of the Beyond as Beyond. It is indirectly experienced in the experience of the finite as finite. Contemplatives are led to recognize that the blocking of all their imaginative and conceptual activity is the impact upon their finite consciousness of the unknown reality of the Unlimited. Hence their experience subjectively is both agony and bliss. There are parallel experiences in the other forms of religion. Social and political action has its dark night, giving rise to a tragic joy or despairing hope.

Moreover, the experience of finitude is a tension that draws us beyond all limits, penetrates and transforms the entirety of human thought and action. It pervades the content of all three cultural spheres and brings about a transvaluation of values. It excludes all evaluations that lock people within the given, whether the given is a system of thought, a revealed deposit of faith, an existing social order or a promised utopia. It also excludes any evaluation that makes the finite self or a finite community, such as the nation, the measure of value. The symbols, practices and rites of religion are thus liberating in so far as they are linked to the negative experience of finitude.

Unfortunately, what is in that way created as the positive content of religion becomes a strong temptation to idolatry. The idolatry comes about in this fashion. The symbols of the Transcendent are taken from each of the three spheres of human culture. Because the Transcendent is immanent, the Beyond also the Depth, its symbols become the animating principles of human culture in its threefold embodiment. But the animating power of the Transcendent is then identified with a particular symbolic content, which is absolutized, instead of being seen in its relationship to a particular form or stage of human culture. The problem is how to retain a continuous basis for the dynamic symbolization of the Transcendent, while remaining open to the constant changes of finite human culture, refusing to absolutize any of its manifestations. So much religion is the mummification of the culturally obsolete.

If, then, for the reasons I have given, we refuse to make religion a distinct cultural sphere, but regard it as the Beyond in the midst of human culture in all its forms, the previous cultural analysis leads us to distinguish three modes of religion, corresponding to the three cultural spheres, which were, we may recall, the cognitive, the normative and the expressive. The cognitive gives rise to cosmic religion, the normative to political religion, the expressive to contemplative religion. The three modes of religion – cosmic, political, contemplative – are distinct but inseparable, just as the three cultural spheres are distinct but inseparable. But one or other mode may be dominant, and thus characterize the religious life of a period or people. However, it should be kept in mind that what I am offering is a typology, which simplifies historical reality for purposes of analysis. What we have in history is the undifferentiated cultures of traditional societies, in which the three modes of religion are entangled, and modern society, which has not yet found how to relate the religion it has inherited to its own differentiated culture. My purpose is to argue that religious people today are making a mistake in confining religion to the third cultural sphere, the expressive, by identifying religious experience with inwardness, and that the primary task is to relate religion to the normative sphere of social and political action.

Let us first, however, consider for a moment the cosmic and contemplative modes of religion. Cosmic religion is a religion as mediated by our knowledge of the external world or cosmos. By extrapolation and analogy, our limited objective knowledge is projected on to the unknown Transcendent. God is worshipped as the creative source and providential sustainer of a cosmic order. The concept of God becomes the representation of total order, the crowning concept of metaphysics, serving as a regulative principle, enabling us to organize the diverse items of our knowledge into a total synthesis or world-view. The medieval conception of the cosmos, which found its supreme articulation in Aquinas, with his synthesis of natural knowledge and revealed doctrine, is the finest example in Christian history of the cosmic mode of religion. What renders it more or less inoperative today is that it claims to know too much, both about God and about the world. (Whiteheadian metaphysics sins in that respect more than Thomism in its authentic form.) We are too aware of the fragmentary nature of our knowledge to attempt the grand synthesis. The modern version of a world-view is an affair of method or procedure rather than of content, which continually changes. There is also a well-grounded reluctance to obscure the peculiar characteristics of religious language by using it in the synthesis with the languages in which we refer to the external world. When the Christian religion is seen as purveying a cosmic synthesis, people are tempted to talk about the Divinity of Christ or about the Trinity as if the use of language in doctrinal statements was the same as in everyday or scientific discourse about the external world.

Hence I expect no grand synthesis between modern knowledge and Christian belief, and I doubt whether the cosmic mode of the Christian religion has anything more than a subordinate role to play in the foreseeable future. We can, I think, no longer look to the cognitive sphere to mediate religious experience to our secular contemporaries. Knowledge has ceased to be the privileged locus for religious faith, and religion has ceased to be plausible in the guise of higher knowledge. Where, then, shall we look next?

The liberal response in the nineteenth century to the desuetude of cosmic religion and the collapse of religion as higher knowledge was to shift the locus of religious experience to the innermost depths of the subject; in other words, from the cognitive to the expressive cultural sphere. The problem of the truth-claims of religious doctrine was obviated, so it was thought, by an appeal to a pre-categorial, pre-linguistic experience. Religious doctrines, together with the other institutional and external elements of religion, are symbolic expressions of the inner experience of the subject. To make objective truth-claims is not in this account their purpose.

The difficulty with that version of religion has been made evident by the linguistic turn in modern thought. There has been a move away from the philosophies of consciousness, away from the Cartesian private subject, with a denial of any unmediated pre-linguistic experience. From that standpoint it would be truer to say that religious experience is the product of religious doctrines, dependent upon the mediation of religious doctrines, than to say that religious doctrines are the product or sedimentation of experience.

The religion of Cartesian subjectivity is only a bastard form of Augustine's religion of inwardness. For Augustine the inner self is a temple in which the person meets God. Descartes' subject is like a spider, drawing everything other than mere matter, including its concept of God, out of its own belly. Modern subjectivism encloses the self upon the self in a claustrophobic fashion, inducing a nihilistic breakdown. In contrast, Augustine, in entering into the self, found it an abyss filled with light from the presence of God. All the same, even for Augustine, God was met not by the expansion of the self into the world other than the self, but by the withdrawal of the self from the world. The Christian West inherited from Augustine the conviction that it was within the self that one met God; that within the depths of the self the union with God was established, sustained and consummated. Religion, properly speaking, was therefore a matter of leaving behind the distracting, multifarious business of the outer world so as (in Newman's words) to 'rest in the thought of two and two only absolute and luminously self-evident beings, myself and my Creator'.

Such a religion of inwardness has an important contribution to make, both culturally and religiously. The differentiation through reflection of the self as individual subject is a condition for the liberation of the self from alienating compulsions, both natural and social. The interior self, or self within, should not indeed be regarded as an isolated or private entity, existing apart from social mediation and communication. The liberated self is a self-conscious subject in possession of his or her individuated being and activities, and thus able to enter as a free participant into the communication process of society. Further, it is understandable that those with religious faith should reflexively apprehend their self as constituted in a relationship with the Transcendent. The distortion, however, that attends this mode of religion is the rejection of the world, of the bodily side of human existence, of the social and the historical. Augustine himself did not avoid that error, but was the main source of its influence upon the West.

But a further point must be added. There is nothing in itself religious about the exploration and cultivation of inner states of consciousness, as found in devotional and mystical treatises. The interior life is no more religious of itself than cosmic synthesis or political action. The inner world of the subject with all its phenomena and ramifications may, like other realms of human existence and culture, become the vehicle of religious experience. But, while it gives rise to a particular mode of religion, it must not be identified with religion. It is religious in so far as it opens out on to the unknown Transcendent, just as a cosmic synthesis is religious for the same reason; and it falls into idolatry, just as cosmic religion does, if it forgets its finiteness and claims a direct apprehension of the Transcendent.

Moreover, contemplative religion does not have a monopoly of reflection. The contrast is not between inwardness and an unthinking dogmatism on the one hand and between inwardness and mindless activism on the other. All three modes of religion include reflection and as religious imply the raising of the mind and heart above the immediate and the finite to the hidden Transcendent. The difference is that contemplative religion finds the presence of the Transcendent in the inner states of consciousness, cosmic religion in the cosmic order and political religion in social reaction.

I come now to the mode of religion, the political, which is related to the second cultural sphere, the normative, and which is religion as embodied in the institutions and practices of society. The last remark makes it evident that all religion has a political dimension in so far as it always occurs in a social and political context. But contemplative religion characteristically withdraws from social and political involvement, and cosmic religion soars above social concern to the higher truths of theology and metaphysics. Political religion is religion as emergent in social and political action.

Nothing could be more absurdly untrue to Christian history than the contention that the Christian religion as embodied institutionally in the Church is apolitical or above politics, so that it is inappropriate to the priestly or clerical state for its members to be involved religiously in political activity. The Christian religion has always been thoroughly political, with social and political action the major vehicle of the distinctively Christian religious experience. Briefly, Christians find God in their neighbour rather than in their inner consciousness or in the cosmos.

Sociologically, the clergy do not constitute an intelligentsia of philosophers or a class of gurus. The clerical state was and is a political institution. It no doubt represents the religious dimension of political life. But the point is that it represents religion politically. The law that excludes the clergy from engaging in politics is not a simple reflection of the meaning of the clerical state. It is an attempt to establish a monopoly of political power in the central authority of the Church. Further, it is usually invoked when the central authority dislikes the political policy and action initiated locally.

It could be argued that monasticism, with its contemplative tradition, and the Western mystical tradition, have origins and features which are not uniquely Christian, and that the non-Christian origins and features are important ones. But if there is one type of religion which, as it is found in the West, has not got these ambiguities and is undeniably Christian, it is the political.

Yahweh from the beginning was a political God. Most of the images and symbols we use of God are social and political in their basic meaning. The mighty acts of God are a series of political events. The prophetic message is a demand for social justice. Jesus died, not because of his inner life of prayer, but because of his impact upon the social order. The Gospel message is centred upon the political symbol of the Kingdom. The earliest Christian creed was 'Jesus is the Lord' – a declaration that takes its meaning from the political order.

The early Christians were a movement of the marginalized and under-privileged. They eventually came to power in the Roman Empire because their movement offered, culturally and politically, what was needed by society. The Christian religion was the animating principle of the unitary social order of the Middle Ages. The medieval papacy was a political institution. I do not deny that it was religious. The point is that it was politically religious. What constituted papal religion was not higher knowledge nor mystical leadership but the contribution it made over the centuries to the formation and development of Christendom or Europe. The reasons for the break-up of Christendom and the gradual secularization of the social and political order of Europe lie not in religion's involvement in politics, but in its identification with bad politics, even to the ignoring or the denial of distinctively Christian values. The problem today is not how to free religion from politics, which would be a harmful privatization of religion, but how to free it from the politics of the past, so that it can make its contribution to the politics of the present and the future.

All the same, culture and politics are not in themselves religious. They only mediate religious truths and values. Society is not to be identified with the Transcendent. But when the presence of the Transcendent in society is acknowledged, it opens the social horizon beyond the limits of any existing order to further possibilities, while acting as the animating but discriminating principle of what already exists.

Since political action is not in itself religious, the question arises: when does it become religious? When does it receive a religious determination? Here I can only sketch the lines of an analysis from a Christian perspective. It calls for expansion, both with regard to its usefulness in the interpretation of past history and in relation to the concrete issues of today.

If Christian performance is constituted as being Christian by being animated by faith, hope and charity, then political action is religiously Christian when (1) it remains in a critical relationship to the existing order; (2) it is utopian in its openness to new possibilities; and (3) it refuses to respond to hate with hate but, instead, embraces the risk of offering gratuitous love. A political refusal to regard any existing social order or set of political institutions as absolute and unchanging is related to faith inasmuch as faith, in being a response to the Infinite, relativizes all finite orders. Faith protects us from the idolatry of worshipping the established order. It is subversive in the awareness it creates of the limitations of all human achievements. The Gospel parables have rightly been called 'subversive stories' in their overthrowing of the worlds we construct for ourselves, with their limited meanings and finite values. In a far more consistent manner than Marxism, a politics animated by Christian faith should express the willingness to enter into a continuous and endless critique of all earthly institutions, beliefs, customs and practices. However, the critique should not be in the name of some new absolute, but under an appeal to the unknown Infinite or Beyond. Too much religion, like the secular ideologies that imitate it, has absolutized its own finite forms.

Besides faith there is hope. The politics of hope rests upon the confidence that, however bleak the prospect, there are always new possibilities. The ability to change direction, to inaugurate and make effective a new policy, is always there. The situation is never hopeless; the outcome is never a foregone conclusion. Christian hope is utopian, not in any unrealistic regard for facts, but in a refusal to measure what can be done by any earthly or purely human calculus. The principle of grace is operative here. It holds that human resources are never adequate to the fulfilment of human destiny, which comes as a gift. Hence our reliance is not upon ourselves, but upon God. Hope keeps the Christian working to bring about change and watching for new opportunities to appear when there would seem to be no grounds for anything other than despair.

It says much for how far the Christian religion has already been privatized, leaving politics amoral as well as secular, that the imperative to respond to hate not with hate but with love is regarded as applicable to personal relationships, but not to politics. Yet the imperative to love first, to love gratuitously and forgivingly, to break the cycle of hate, to return good for evil, not evil for evil, is basic to the Christian understanding of the fallen human condition and the gift of salvation. It applies as much to politics and society as to individual relationships. Socially as well as individually, if what we call love is a mere self-interested calculus of gains and losses, we shall inevitably be caught in a downward spiral of cumulative hate. That spiral can be broken only if we are prepared to give without an assured return. To do that requires an openness to the gift of God's creative love. There is debate today whether the Christian imperative of love demands a policy of non-violence. One can leave that question open, provided one recognizes that even in the hypothesis that violent resistance is both allowable and necessary for Christians in society, such violence must never be motivated by hate, but always controlled and limited by love.

Those, then, are a few brief indications of a Christian transformation of politics. To transform politics in that fashion constitutes a political mode of religious practice and experience. Social interaction thus opens out upon the Transcendent and mediates an experience of the Beyond. The response to that experience is the animation of political activity with Christian values. But I want to do more than defend the legitimacy of the political mode of religious faith. I would argue that social and political activity is today the privileged locus of religious experience. The reason is that contemporary society is struggling with a strong temptation to turn its back upon the poor and the weak for a policy of self-interest unrestrained by compassion. Because the welfare state has run into economic difficulties, the powerful are protecting their own interests with a cynical disregard for the victims. The rich are becoming richer and the poor poorer on both the national and international level. At the same time, an illusory search for an unattainable ultimate security is producing a suicidal reliance upon nuclear arms. In this situation Christians cannot withdraw into a religion of inwardness and watch the remnants of Christian society being swamped by an egoistic individualism. They are called upon to mediate a healing grace that will purify, guide and restrain the working of self-interest in human affairs and then further to transform those affairs by relating them to a transcendent order of values. That is the religious performance imposed upon us by the signs of the time. It is there we find the primary locus for religious experience today. An appeal to a supposed primacy of contemplative religion, combined with a collusion with the existing social and political order, is the major temptation at present for religious people, especially for those in authority.

CHAPTER 4

The Christian question to radicalism

In the context of my argument in the previous chapter that social and political activity is today the privileged locus of religious experience, I want to ask how far radicalism is compatible with the Christian faith. Christian belief in a transcendent Kingdom as the ultimate fulfilment of human solidarity imposes limits to what can be expected from politics in seeking fundamental change in human society. But first, since radicalism is an unusually vague term, I must make clear the meaning I have in mind.

In the widest sense, 'radical' is used of those political and religious views that push to an extreme their demand for change in the existing order. It is generally associated with a movement for fundamental change, but the exact change desired has differed from period to period. Moreover, although most often used of left-wing democratic movements, 'radicalism' does sometimes designate right-wing oligarchical movements calling for a regeneration of society.

My concern is with a more precise meaning. By radicalism I mean the belief that human reason and will are powerful enough to overcome the present imperfection of the human condition by basic social and political change and thus to create a completely new social order of liberty, equality and fraternity. There are several elements in the definition.

First, there is the idea that social and political change, if thorough enough, can remove the present evils of the human condition. This reflects the gradual weakening and loss of belief in the doctrine of original sin. From the Renaissance onwards, there was a reluctance to accept that human beings were intrinsically implicated in a reign of sin and thus in permanent need of a supernatural redemption. Human nature was regarded as good, and men and women as capable of improving their condition. It was Rousseau who first pointed to society as the source of human misery, so that the present evils of the human condition were due to a corrupt social organization. He himself did not think that the situation could be righted by political action, but this was the conclusion drawn by a line of radical thinkers. Hence, radicalism, according to this first element, is the view that the evils of the present human condition are due to a bad, unjust organization of society and that these evils can be removed and human potentiality fully released by social and political action.

The second element is already implied in the first. To make it explicit, it is that reason and will are sufficient of themselves to bring about the changes required in the social order to perfect society, remove present evils and thus achieve fulfilment for human nature. On this point, secular radicalism differs from apocalyptic, which in its extreme demand for fundamental change is the religious counterpart of political radicalism. Apocalyptic radicalism, however, looks not to human power, but to a divine intervention to accomplish the change. Nevertheless, the two may coincide if radical reformers see themselves as instruments of a divine purpose. At the same time, the optimistic confidence in human reason for effecting human improvement and creating a new social order links radicalism to the liberal tradition and the Enlightenment. From that standpoint, for example, John W. Derry in his book, *The Radical Tradition*, can include such unquestionably liberal thinkers as Jeremy Bentham and John Stuart Mill.[1] Radicalism, however, as distinct from liberalism, derives less from the reasonableness of bourgeois thinking than from the vivid example of the practice of the French revolutionaries, who

[1]   John W. Derry, *The Radical Tradition: Tom Paine to Lloyd George* (London: Macmillan, 1967).

showed that sweeping changes could indeed be brought about in the social order by human action. According to the second element, then, radicalism is the confidence that men and women can devise and construct an ideal social order to meet the needs of human fulfilment.

The third element further distinguishes radicalism from liberalism. The radicals were those who refused to go along with the liberals in their individualist stress upon freedom because the liberals ignored or regarded as inevitable the economic inequities of a liberal social order. The radical interpretation of freedom placed it in the context of equality and, in the political order, of democracy. Although the push towards extreme change has often led radicals to the acceptance of dictatorial power on the part of a charismatic leader or select group, the radical vision of the ideal society is egalitarian, and this creates a reluctance to grant that human fulfilment may be mediated by a traditional authority. So, according to the third element, radicalism is an insistence that the essential equality of human beings should result in an equal participation in the economic, social and political life of the ideal social order.

How do each of these elements stand up when compared with the Christian understanding of the human condition and its need for salvation? I take it for granted that the Christian tradition, like any other religious tradition, is not a static deposit, but is open to change and modification within the historical process. Thus, we should not canonize as immutable truth Augustine's view of original sin, despite its dominance of Western culture for centuries. There is no valid objection to loosening up our interpretation of the myth of the Fall, to taking it as a set of symbols, provoking and facilitating reflection upon the human situation in regard to evil, but without its providing a definitive theoretical answer. It would therefore be an exaggeration to argue that human sinfulness excludes the radical aspiration after a fundamentally new social order. There is no reason why the human race should not learn to create institutional checks against the worst manifestation of human waywardness. Indeed, unless this is not merely possible but also actually accomplished in the near future in respect of war, the human race will be exterminated in a nuclear holocaust. The present stress by Christian theologians upon the universality of grace does not allow us to regard the majority of the human race, with Augustine, as a *massa damnata*. Even if the final Kingdom, with its elimination of sin, is not to be fully realized in this historical order, men and women with the help of grace should be able to create a social order closer to the ideal than present society. Christians indeed will differ among themselves in determining how this is to be done and what reforms are practicable in a particular situation. Not all Christians will take the same political option.

To give an example where the Christian outlook straddles the political options, Edmund Burke,[2] the great conservative thinker, argued that revolutions achieve the opposite of what they intend. They begin by promising freedom, equality, justice and democracy, and end in a tyranny that negates all four. The reason is that revolution threatens or produces anarchy. The basic social need is for law and order, for security. Most people, however low their state, fear disorder. They therefore distrust the radicals, who make great promises but who will probably bring chaos. Consequently, radicals usually end by despising the people and imposing their new social order by force. It is difficult to be a radical and a democrat, because extreme measures are usually unpopular. Hence the law put forward by Burke, which states that revolution, or the practical implementation of radical political theory, necessarily leads to tyranny via anarchy. Radicals are led into tyranny because they want to change society fundamentally and fast. But they are also acting, according to Burke, on inadequate knowledge. Radicals have an excessive trust in their theories. There is never in fact enough sufficiently reliable knowledge about the social order with its complexity to justify tearing down an existing order and constructing something entirely new. Politically we must

[2] I am dependent here upon the interpretation of Burke in Michael Freeman, *Edmund Burke and the Critique of Political Radicalism* (Oxford: Basil Blackwell, 1980).

always act with restraint because of the inevitable limits of our knowledge.

There is a great deal to be said in support of Burke's argumentation against revolution. Its weakness is that the scenario Burke presupposes is not always verified in fact. His scenario is that of a stable, if unjust, society which is threatened by anarchy because revolutionaries are acting to overthrow the existing order and replace it by a new and more just order. But the factual situation may be that the social order has already disintegrated through the misrule of the governing class, who in the absence of a rule of law are clinging to their privileges by terrorism and uncontrolled oppression. The ordinary people may be deprived of the basic security, which any society is intended to supply, because they are subject to arbitrary arrest and the lack of the basic material necessities of life. Revolutionary action in those circumstances is not the overthrow of the social order, but an attempt to restore social order by action – from below. In extreme situations only extreme measures may work; moderate action may not even be possible.

In any particular instance the situation will rarely be crystal clear. Hence it will be differently assessed by people whose fundamental political attitudes differ. In brief, there will be the political conservatives, urging moderation, and political radicals, insisting that matters have become intolerable. There may be Christians in both groups. It is a mistake to suppose that the differences can be settled by appealing to traditional Christian teaching or by an authoritative decree of the ecclesiastical hierarchy. A factual assessment and a practical judgement are involved here. These will be influenced by a person's hold upon Christian meanings and values, and Christians in the local community affected by the situation should endeavour to reach a sufficient consensus for some degree of common policy and action. This may not always be possible, but Christians have to learn to differ from one another in practical social and political affairs without immediately labelling their opponents un-Christian.

All the same, if Christian faith is not to be emptied of content, the meanings and values it carries with it must at times clash with those implied in one or other political option. Where differences are rooted in a divergent factual assessment and in estimating the probable effects of action, Christians fully unified in faith may differ. But this is not so where the differences are differences of fundamental outlook. If political radicalism is not taken simply to mean the advocacy of revolutionary action in extreme situations, but is made explicit as a fundamental political theory, consisting of the elements I have analysed, there is cause to ask about its compatibility with any recognizable version of the Christian understanding of the human condition. That kind of questioning should not be raised only in regard to radicalism; it is in place concerning liberalism and conservatism as basic political options. But it comes to the fore with radicalism, because for some the radical option has taken on the lineaments of a secular religion, and some Christians, judging rightly that being a Christian in the present un-Christian world involves social and political action to change the world, have been tempted to identify Christianity with political radicalism.

Political radicalism does, I suggest, clash in several fundamental respects with Christian principles. I am indeed treating radical ideas in the abstract. How far they are actually held by political radicals will have to be determined in particular instances. The ideas, however, are sufficiently current to call for a theoretical clarification. The various ways in which radicalism clashes with Christian principle may be summed up by saying that radicalism transgresses the limits that Christianity imposes upon political action.

Take the first element of radicalism, namely, the conviction that the evils of the human condition can be removed and human potentiality fully released by social and political action. Since Christian faith relates human beings to God as transcendent reality, the subject of Christian faith and the recipient of Christian salvation must be seen as transcending any historical social and political order.

The subject of Christian faith is, from one standpoint, the individual person, actualized in his or her individuality by the response to God's call that every individual must make for himself or herself, because it cannot be made vicariously by another. That is the essence of Christian individualism, which places each individual in a personal relationship with God. From another standpoint, the subject of Christian faith is the community constituted by persons who, in opening themselves to a relationship with God, have thereby opened themselves to one another. Faith in actualizing the individual constitutes the community or Kingdom of God. It is, however, a community that cannot be fully identified with an institutional community. From a sociological viewpoint, it is a community-forming principle rather than a community. The recipient of Christian salvation is the communal individual as freed from sin and as immortalized, that is, having overcome death, however that victory is more precisely interpreted.

But if such is the subject of Christian faith and salvation, that subject, that faith, that salvation, cannot be brought within the confines of any temporal social order. No matter how ideal may be a society, it cannot in its own temporal terms provide faith to ward off ultimate meaninglessness and salvation to overcome sin and death. I say 'in its own temporal terms', because social and political institutions and action may, especially when sacred and secular have not yet been clearly differentiated, have a function in mediating faith and salvation. Again, because of the interdependence of the various levels of human existence, it is not true to say that no matter how bad and unjust a society may be, men and women in it may still always meet God in faith and receive salvation from him. The evils of society may and often do block people's access to the higher levels of human existence. What is true is that faith and the conscious acceptance of salvation do not demand an ideal order of society and can be found even in a high degree where social conditions are far from ideal. In brief, society on the level of social and political organization is neither the cause nor the remedy for the fundamental ills of the human condition, and it is not the source of human fulfilment at its deepest level, even though it may act negatively to block or positively to mediate access to that source.

Admittedly, then, there is an extrinsic dependence of faith

and salvation upon social and political conditions. If a person is starving, one must first give him or her food before talking about saving souls. In general, the injustice of a social and political regime in depriving people of the satisfaction of their basic needs – for self-esteem and community, not just for food and shelter – will, apart from a miracle of grace, block the emergence of the higher needs and aspirations proper to a developed human life. The establishment of basic social justice and of a political order free from stark oppression may be the necessary path in the bringing of faith and salvation. Again, it is a mistake to suppose that religious activity is necessarily private and personal. Actions embodying religious meaning and values are as appropriate in the public realm as in that of private existence. All the same, human society in the variety of its historical forms and in the different degrees of its success in satisfying human social needs does not belong to the deepest level of human existence, where human beings are related to a transcendent order. In making society the root of human evil and the place of human fulfilment, political radicalism distorts politics by disguised religion.

The second element of political radicalism, namely the confidence in human ability to construct an ideal social order, likewise offends against political modesty. Let us suppose that the social order has been brought to a peak of perfection. As a temporal order, it will remain subject to change, which if perfection has indeed been reached will be in the direction of disintegration and corruption. The historical process does not allow eternal permanence. But the more striking defect of any utopia built by human hands is that it provides for the fulfilment only of the generation that achieves it and for those subsequent generations that precede its eventual collapse. It has nothing to offer the victims of generation after generation of preceding history. More than that, it would seem that the ideal social order, made immanent in history without transcendence, can offer human fulfilment only at the cost of a complete forgetfulness of the victims of past history. To remember them would be to evoke a frustrated sense of human solidarity, which would either mar with sadness the utopian fulfilment or be repressed with a blunting of human sensibility. There is indeed an inherent absurdity in a secular radicalism which calls for generation after generation to work for a fulfilment they themselves will never enjoy, while at the same time repudiating the self-transcending faith that alone would ground such selfless action. If, as a radical, one is dissatisfied with the politics of enlightened self-interest and yearns for the achievement of human solidarity, one is led to hope for a communion among human beings that transcends both space and time. We cannot forget the victims of the past. As Walter Benjamin noted, people are moved 'by the image of enslaved ancestors rather than that of liberated grandchildren'.[3] But however envisaged, such a transcendent communion is not within the range of political action. Hence, though hope for it will transform political action away from self-interest towards concern for others in justice and love, it will inculcate an acute sense of the limits of political action that will moderate the urge to create a new social order by political means.

The alternative to consciously reconstructing radicalism as a religious rather than a political hope is to turn it into a tragic vision of human history, according to which human beings can only find fragments of human meaning by working for the ideals of freedom and justice with the realization that the human enterprise is in any event destined to end in extermination, meaninglessness and nothingness. Radical politics without any ultimate meaning! It is indeed a possible option, but it is essentially a religious not a political option, to be assessed accordingly.

The third element of political radicalism is its egalitarianism. In so far as this was historically an uncovering of the brutal economic inequality that was veiled by the bourgeois ideology of freedom, it was a legitimate political demand. But in so far as equality is erected into a universal political principle, it implies an attempt to extend human control beyond its appropriate range. Human beings are unequal in the endowments of nature

---

[3] From the 'Theses on the philosophy of history', in Walter Benjamin, *Illuminations*, ed. and introduction by Hannah Arendt (Glasgow: Fontana/Collins, 1973), p. 262.

and in the gifts of God's grace. Although the limited human control over nature may do something to offset the inequalities of natural endowment, it is questionable whether this should be done in the name of equality. That, as experience shows, is most likely to lead to a levelling down rather than a levelling up, an impoverishment rather than an enrichment. In any event, human beings have no control over the gifts of the Spirit and over the utterly free distribution of God's grace. Undoubtedly, for the Christian, human beings are essentially equal in the sense that each person stands before God as having eternal, individual worth. Hence, each person is an end and cannot ever legitimately be treated as a mere means. Moreover, personal worth is not to be measured by the function of place the human occupies in earthly society. For that reason, radicality has fundamentally relativized social and political inequalities. All the same, the radical vision does not see human beings as equal, either by nature or by grace. It allows, therefore, a place for authority or legitimate power over others in both political and religious institutions. The drive for equality, religiously assessed, is an arrogant claim by human beings to total mastery over their destiny. So often its consequence is the urge to destroy what persists in eluding human control.

To bring these remarks to some conclusion, if radicalism is understood in a broad, vague sense as the conviction that in a particular situation the existing order of society must be fundamentally changed, it is a practical judgement and decision that is not merely compatible with Christian faith but may also be based upon its values. Our present society is both structurally un-Christian and headed for annihilation. Christians, therefore, are called upon to work for its fundamental change. But radicalism may be viewed as more than a practical response to a particular situation, as a theoretical political option, a set of political principles, determining a conception of society, of human perfectibility, of human destiny. The three elements I have analysed constitute a political theory, present in various forms on the political scene since at least the French Revolution. As such it forms a political outlook incompatible with Christian faith for reasons I have stated. If I have stressed the incompatibility of radicalism rather than of, say, bourgeois liberalism, it is to make clear the distinction between a firm Christian commitment to social and political action in favour of the oppressed and exploited and its deceptive similitude, namely, a political radicalism that identifies human fulfilment with the establishment of an ideal social and political order.

PART II

Praxis, narrative and religious language

CHAPTER 5

Theology and praxis

Theology has been traditionally understood as the interpretation of a previously given faith. *Fides quaerens intellectum* (faith seeking understanding) is its tag. Faith for many Christians has been taken as doctrinal, and theology is then seen as the interpretation of a set of truths, written in Scripture and handed down in tradition. Where, however, in reaction against an intellectual account of faith as assent to propositions, faith is regarded as a personal meeting with God as revealing himself in Christ, theology then becomes the reflexive apprehension of this faith encounter. But in either case theology is the interpretation of a pre-given religious reality, an already existing reality regarded as remaining essentially identical with itself in history. Theology would thus presuppose the unbroken self-identity of faith through all the changes of human society.

A twofold problem arises here. How in that case does theology avoid being an acceptance of, at least an acquiescence in, the present human situation? Is it not inevitably compromised as a rationalization, an attempted legitimation, of past and present human society, covering up or mystifying the alienation that society has brought? The history of faith and the history of human society merge into one history. To approach that history merely by way of interpretation is to conceive it as transmitting meaning and truth. But is it not in fact a history of alienation, a place of unmeaning and untruth, a story of domination and repression? If one tries to meet this objection by saying that theology in expressing faith formulates a protest against the present human condition and the oppressions of society, then one falls into the second half of the problem. The difficulty here is the claim of faith to remain identical with itself, pure and undefiled, amid the changes of society. Such a claim to constitute an independent realm of truth would seem to be a deceptive denial of the actual social basis of faith. It makes faith an ideology, a reflection of social domination, because to deny or be unaware of the dependence of all forms of consciousness upon the social order is to be more than ever its victim. Faith, together with theology, cannot be genuinely a protest against the social order unless it acknowledges that it itself and its own past history as the product of alienated society must be submitted to criticism and revolutionary transformation. It cannot place itself apart and, prior to criticism, claim an unchanging self-identity.

Most will have recognized the echo of Marx in what I have just said. I am indeed drawing upon Marx's critique of philosophy and religion. Let me recall the famous eleventh thesis on Feuerbach: 'The philosophers have only *interpreted* the world, in various ways; the point, however, is to *change* it'.[1] Again, in *The German Ideology*, Marx and Engels, referring to the Young Hegelians with their conviction that all that was needed was a change of consciousness, remarked: 'This amounts to a demand to interpret what exists in a different way, that is, to recognize it by means of a different interpretation'.[2] To remain on the hermeneutical level – in other words, to engage in a process of reinterpretation – is to acknowledge the tradition interpreted as essentially meaningful. But existing social traditions have to be explained and transcended, not interpreted. In the texts quoted, Marx is speaking of philosophy – in particular of Hegelianism. But he describes theology as 'ever the infected spot of philosophy',[3]

[1] Lewis S. Feuer, ed., *Karl Marx and Friedrich Engels: Basic Writings on Politics and Philosophy* (New York: Doubleday, 1959), p. 245 (Feuer's italics).
[2] Lloyd D. Easton and Kurt H. Guddat, eds., *Writings of the Young Marx on Philosophy and Society* (New York: Doubleday, 1967), p. 408.
[3] Economic and Philosophical Manuscripts, Preface. See T. B. Bottomore, ed., *Karl Marx: Early Writings* (New York, Toronto and London: McGraw-Hill, 1964), p. 65.

and for him theology or religion was the ideological component, or better the disease, of philosophy. It was precisely in so
far as it remained a hidden theology that philosophy was
ideology, namely the formulation of class interest as universal
truth. But whereas philosophy, according to Marx, is to be
realized by its negation or abolition (*Aufhebung*) in a unity of
theory and *praxis*, religion or theology cannot be realized by
being negated in its present state. It is ideology through and
through and is destined merely to disappear. What characterized thought as religious for Marx was its being mere theory
divorced from social practice. By claiming permanent and
universal truth in theory as if it were independent of social
conditions, religion uncritically reflected patterns of social
dominance and concealed social reality in mystifying
abstractions.

The Marxist critique of religion, therefore, is by no means
answered by deploring the social inaction of the Church in the
nineteenth century and by urging Christians to work for social
reform in the twentieth. What is rejected by Marx is any claim
to have access to truth other than through an activity directed
to transforming society. We cannot anticipate the historical
process. We possess the degree of truth belonging to the present
stage in the development of human society. To suppose a once-
for-all revelation, to anticipate that faith will remain identical
with itself, is for Marx to fall into ideology because it is in effect
a denial of concrete history and an escape into abstraction.

A great difference in structure separates Marxist thinking
from traditional Catholic theology, which is dogmatic in faith
and Aristotelian in philosophy. A first insight into this structural contrast may be given by this passage from Lobkowicz's
study, *Theory and Practice: History of a Concept from Aristotle to
Marx*:

Aristotle philosophizes out of 'wonder', out of an intellectual curiosity
which is half awe, half the desire to adjust man's existence to the order
of being, the cosmos. Both Hegel and Marx, on the contrary,
philosophize out of unhappiness and dissatisfaction, out of the
'experience' that the world is not as it ought to be. Accordingly, while
Aristotle primarily aims at understanding, at discovering structures

and laws to which man's [and woman's] thought and actions have to
adjust, Hegel and Marx aim at 'reconciling' and/or 'revolutionizing'.
In Aristotle nothing is or even can be wrong as it is in its natural state.
The problem for Aristotle does not consist in correcting the universe
or in making it rational; it consists in discovering its inherent order
and rationality and in adjusting oneself to it. In Hegel and Marx
almost everything is wrong and consequently has to be *aufgehoben*,
transfigured, transformed, revolutionized. In this respect the only
truly important difference between Hegel and Marx is that Hegel is
still enough committed to the Greek philosophical tradition to believe
it possible to reconcile man with the universe by teaching him
adequately to understand it, while Marx, disappointed with Hegel's
speculative transfiguration, has lost all faith in the healing and
reconciling power of mere thought.[4]

There are two points here. First, Marx's apprehension of the
world as wrong excludes the contemplative acquiescence of
reality of traditional theology. Second, Marx's loss of faith in
the power of mere thought excludes all attempts to modernize
theology by way of reinterpretation.

To pause over the second point. Alasdair MacIntyre at the
end of his *Marxism and Christianity* made the comment: 'Nothing
has been more startling than to note how much contemporary
Christian theology is concerned with trying to perform Feuerbach's work all over again'.[5] In other words, what modern
theology, whether Protestant or Catholic, has been doing is
giving the Christian faith a secular meaning or at least a secular
relevance by a reinterpretation that supposedly disentangled its
true, essential content. Thus, we have had the theologies of
secularization from Gogarten to Van Buren and Harvey Cox,
Bultmann's demythologizing, the death-of-God theologies, the
progressive theologies of the Catholic liberals. The affinity of all
these with Feuerbach's work is not far-fetched. Feuerbach, it
will be remembered, claimed to be uncovering the essential
meaning of Christianity, its true anthropological essence.
Although his interpretation was atheistic and anti-theological,
it was not in Marx's radical sense irreligious.

[4] Nicholas Lobkowicz, *Theory and Practice: History of a Concept from Aristotle to Marx*
(Notre Dame, IN, and London: University of Notre Dame Press, 1967), pp. 340–1.
[5] Alasdair MacIntyre, *Marxism and Christianity* (Harmondsworth: Penguin, 1968), p.
106.

Or, rather, the trouble with Feuerbach, as with the modern theology after him, is his failure to step outside the abstract, ideal, merely theoretical enclosure of religion into the concrete historical reality of society with its relationships and contradictions. Underlying the demand to reinterpret religion is the basic demand to change society. Merely to reinterpret is to neglect the main task; it is to leave things as they are and indeed enter into a complicity with the unsatisfactory situation that gave rise to what the reinterpretation strives to transcend.

Marx's criticism of Feuerbach applies easily to much modern theology. I should like to quote his fourth thesis on Feuerbach in full, so that it can be read with modern theology and its criticism of traditional supernaturalist other-worldly religion in mind:

Feuerbach starts out from the fact of religious self-alienation, the duplication of the world into a religious, imaginary world and a real one. His work consists in the dissolution of the religious world into its secular basis. He overlooks the fact that after completing this work, the chief thing still remains to be done. For the fact that the secular foundation detaches itself from itself and establishes itself in the clouds as an independent realm is really to be explained only by the self-cleavage and self-contradictoriness of this secular basis. The latter must itself, therefore, first be understood in its contradiction and then, by the removal of the contradiction, revolutionized in practice. Thus, for instance, once the earthly family is discovered to be the secret of the holy family, the former must then itself be criticized in theory and revolutionized in practice.[6]

But if that is applied to modern secularizing theology, the question arises: can theology move from being a critique of religion to being a critique of secular reality, a critique bound up with revolutionary *praxis*, without ceasing to be theology?

To define the problematic of critical theology more closely something must first be said about the relation of theory and *praxis* in Marx.

In the late 1830s the Young Hegelians were faced with the problem of going beyond the system of Hegel, the supreme form of theory. There was a vague feeling that thought was not

---

[6] Feuer, ed., *Karl Marx and Friedrich Engels*, p. 244.

enough. At this juncture, in 1838, August von Cieszkowski published a small book in German, entitled *Prologomena zur Historiosophie*. Cieszkowski still admitted that in Hegel, philosophy had reached its culmination. But even absolute knowledge was not enough; reconciliation at the level of thought must be completed by a reconciliation at the level of action. The role of philosophy was to become a practical philosophy, exercising a direct influence on social life and developing the future by concrete activity. Hegel's philosophy marked a turning-point: before Hegel practice had preceded consciousness; now practice was post-theoretical, conscious of itself through and through, a synthesis of Being and Thought. For this post-theoretical activity, Cieszkowski used the word 'praxis', thus introducing a term destined to become widely influential. The word in Greek, having the ordinary meaning of action or doing, takes on the more technical sense of ethical and political activity in Aristotle. Although Cieszkowski's book was not widely read – there is no clear evidence that Marx ever read it – it made available a useful concept at the right moment. Admittedly, as Bernstein remarks: 'Among the left Hegelians, the excitement generated by talk of "praxis" was equalled only by the vagueness with which they used the expression'.[7] But it reflected and helped the secularization and politicization among the Young Hegelians, the shift from theology to politics, and provided the context for the development of Marx.

Praxis in Marx covers a wide range of human activity, from bodily labour and production to political revolution. It includes criticism and theoretical activity. The common characteristic constituting human activities as *praxis* is their power to transform reality and society and make them more human. Only those activities contributing to the humanization of men and women are *praxis* in the strict sense.

Marx rejected the idealism of Hegel and with it the ultimate identity of subject and object. His materialism was an insistence upon reality as independent of mind. But Marx did not set up

[7] Richard J. Bernstein, *Praxis and Action: Contemporary Philosophies of Human Activity* (Philadelphia: University of Pennsylvania Press, 1971), p. xi.

an opposing metaphysics, with Matter instead of Spirit as ultimate principle. For him, nature was mediated only through the concrete history of human society. Matter was the objective, non-identical component met with in labour. For Marx, what existed in the last analysis was only the human being bound to nature through labour. At the basic level, then, there is the process of productive labour as the interrelationship and interaction of human beings with nature. This productive process gives rise to the relationships that constitute society and to the various forms of consciousness. The human's relationship to nature through labour is historical in the sense that it develops. Concrete history is not the history of consciousness, but of human beings in varying and developing relations of productive labour. In the course of history contradictions arise. Human beings have become alienated from their labour and the product of their labour, from themselves and their fellows. Humanizing activity or *praxis* is therefore revolutionary *praxis*, directed to the changing of economic and social relationships.

One can truly say that for Marx the only source of meaning in the universe is *praxis*. But what about theory? First, however, it is necessary to introduce the notion of critique.

Cieszkowski's *praxis* was not critical, but the activity of a humanity which, having reached absolute knowledge, now proceeds to organize society according to it. Bauer,[8] however, beginning with Christianity, insisted upon the need of a series of critiques which would unmask the irrationality of everything opposed to absolute knowledge. To unmask the irrational was to destroy it. Therefore Bauer maintained that true practice is precisely critical theory. This belief in the power of a purely theoretical criticism was mocked by Marx and Engels in *The Holy Family* and *The German Ideology*.

Bauer's critique, like Cieszkowski's *praxis*, flowed from absolute knowledge as reached by Hegel's philosophy. What Marx saw was that a total, supposedly all-embracing philosophy like Hegel's fell into contradiction with itself as soon as it became

---

[8] For a brief account of Bruno Bauer and his thought see Karl Löwith, *From Hegel to Nietzsche: The Revolution in 18th Century Thought* (New York: Doubleday, 1987), pp. 339–46.

critical. To criticize was to concede that something was not what it ought to be according to the philosophy, that it was outside the philosophy or unphilosophical. Hence Marx's conviction that to actualize philosophy was to negate it and go beyond it. The realization of philosophy was its abolition.

Marx, therefore, establishes a unity of theory and *praxis*. Theory is the consciousness of *praxis*; *praxis* is action infused with and made conscious by theory. Marx rejected the notion of theory independent of *praxis*, theory as presuppositionless, contemplative recognition of a stable object. Indeed, any theory claiming such independence was ideology, all the more the mystifying reflection of existing society the more it claimed an illusory independence. Theoretical activity, like the practical activity with which it is one, is a product of the changing reality of society and of the relationship with nature mediated by society. Theory, therefore, develops as society develops; theory is affected by alienation when the social order is alienating. Critical theory is the conscious component of revolutionary *praxis*, a theoretical consciousness inseparable from the concrete, historical effort to overcome the contradictions in existing society and thus create a world more in accord with the needs and potentialities of men and women.

It must be stressed that Marx does not measure our present alienated state against a normative, transhistorical human nature nor against a future, logically predetermined ideal. He does not put forward an explanation of the world, of its origin and end. That would be to fall back into the theoretical philosophy he rejected. What he offers is a critical analysis, but an analysis that uncovers not only what is but also what ought to be. According to Marx it is a correct understanding of the present alienated state that reveals human potentialities. In other words, an analysis of existing society, in particular political economy, enables us to envisage previously unknown possibilities for human actualization. Marx did not accept the dichotomy of fact and value. Human alienation was an objective condition; to understand it was to discover the human's potentiality for a social order more in harmony with human needs and power. But any speculation about future possibilities not grounded in a critical analysis of present society was empty. Further, while critical theory infused revolutionary *praxis* and made it conscious, the transformation effected by *praxis* in turn changed theory by altering its basis. Theory and *praxis* march in step. Moreover, contradictions met with in theory cannot be overcome by theory alone, but only through the transformation of the social basis achieved in *praxis*.

In this context we can better understand the Marxian concept of ideology. Ideology reflects the world as wrong, as afflicted with contradictions and alienation, but does not uncover its wrongness; it conceals or mystifies it. The ideological reflection is both true and false. It is true inasmuch as it reflects the actual situation; it is false inasmuch as it does not reveal its wrongness. Critical science, on the contrary, depicts the reality of the situation in such a way as to reveal its wrongness and uncover a potentiality for revolutionary transformation.

Such, then, is the flexible, non-dogmatic Marxism reconstructed by the interpreters of the Frankfurt School. They go on to argue that Marx's critique of political economy is inadequate to the present phase of capitalism and what is now needed is a critique of technocracy. But to modify the Marxist analysis, they maintain, is to follow the Marxist understanding of the relation between theory and *praxis*.

Marx carried out his critique of bourgeois society by a critique of the reflection of that society in the bourgeois science of political economy. The same procedure is being adopted by those theologians who are trying to establish a critical theology, namely a theology that accepts the Marxist unity of theory and *praxis*. In other words, critical theology is conceived as the critique of theology. Through a critique of existing theology, the unmasking of its ideological distortions, the possibility of future development may be revealed. Let us trace some of the lines of this critique, first taking up the question of theological positivism.

Positivism here designates the attitude that makes assertions *a priori*, with violence or defiance, while refusing any mediation of critical reason. It coincides with dogmatism. What is objectionable is not the admission of a positive datum, like the event of Jesus Christ or the reality of the Christian Church, as the starting point of faith, but the attempt to impose it uncritically by authority alone. This results in the identification of the given reality with a particular set of concepts considered as embodying it. No account is taken of the limits and demands of the process of knowledge. The concepts formed at a particular time in the history of faith are turned into fetishes, abstracted from their historical roots in human society and making their claim upon us by an authority unmediated by our human reality.

As pre-critical, positivism is in effect pre-Kantian. The word 'critical' still carries the Kantian sense of a self-reflective examination of the limits and validity of knowledge. As Jeremy Shapiro put it,

Kant's critique of reason, by formulating the experiences of self-reflection, dissolved the seemingly compelling necessity of the world that man had gradually built up about himself ... the Kantian revolution, by liberating reflection as a weapon against pre-given reality, changed the very structure of history. That is why it is not possible to go back behind Kant – not without re-entering a mythical world in which man [or woman] has abdicated his [or her] potential for freedom and the construction of a rational world.[9]

Since Bonhoeffer dubbed neo-orthodoxy a positivism of revelation, the word 'positivism' has been chiefly associated in theology with Karl Barth. Karl Barth was much concerned with Feuerbach's anti-theology and argued that any mediation of faith through human knowledge inevitably led to Feuerbach's reduction of theology to anthropology. The only way to avoid Feuerbach's critique was to set faith apart as discontinuous with human reason. But Barth did not escape the trap of identifying faith with his own version of it. In fact, the structure of his thought corresponded with that of Feuerbach himself, since the latter, as Xhaufflaire points out, was also a positivist, although differing in what he identified as the unquestionable *a priori* of all thought. But whether reason, the human species, or nature with Feuerbach, or the word of God with Barth is made

9   Jeremy J. Shapiro, 'From Marcuse to Habermas', *Continuum*, 9 (1971), pp. 65–6.

absolute, there is essentially the same attempt to freeze human history with a fetish.

The word 'positivist' may rightly be applied also to that tendency among Catholics to secure the continuation of the Church by the mere repetition and authoritarian reproduction of traditional formulations and institutions. According to this model, all who belong to the Church must adhere without reservation to the confession of faith as interpreted by authority and mould their lives upon the officially promulgated moral code. To insist upon this positivist model without compromise would in modern society give the Church the characteristics of a sect. In earlier periods a sect embodied a dynamic conflict with the wider society and the established Churches. But for the Church today to adopt the structure of a sect in an attempt to immobilize the effects of the social dynamism of modern society upon itself would not represent a fruitful confrontation but an attempt to escape reality. The authorities of the Catholic Church see well enough that they would lose their hold upon men and women today if they refused all change. Hence positivism has now been tempered with a measure of secularization and is found in an uncompromising form only in the small conservative groups of right-wing Catholics, where sectarian characteristics are unmistakable.[10]

We pass next to what may be called in a general sense theologies of mediation. The phrase is used here to designate the work of those theologians who do not regard the positive givenness of faith and tradition as excluding the functioning of philosophical and scientific reason and indeed insist upon the part played by human rationality in the appropriation of faith and tradition. Against all who, like Feuerbach, would reduce religion to secular reality, the effort of these theologies is to establish the truth and validity of a distinctively religious experience, which, it is then contended, is made explicit and concrete in Christianity. But any theology of mediation in modern times must also include the exercise of critical reason upon the Bible and upon the past tradition and formulations of

[10] Cf. M. Xhaufflaire, 'L'Eglise du demain', *Lumière et Vie*, 19 (1970), pp. 134–5.

the Christian faith. There is thus a mediation in the present between the past and the future, that is, between the traces left by the past history of faith and the possibilities uncovered for its creative continuation.

A Catholic example of a theology of mediation is the theology of Karl Rahner. I will limit my comments upon his vast *œuvre* to his presentation of a practical theology of the Church in her present existence as given in the five-volume *Handbuch der Pastoraltheologie*,[11] of which he is one of the editors and contributors. (The sub-title is *Praktische Theologie der Kirche in ihrer Gegenwart*.) That is the place where we find expressed his understanding of the relation of theology to practice and to social reality as reflected in the social sciences.

An analysis of the valiant attempt of Rahner and his collaborators to create a genuinely practical theology for the concrete action of the Church today shows an underlying assumption, simply taken for granted, which affects the entire structure of the enterprise. What is assumed is a distinction between the permanent essence of the Church and its phenomenal existence, between the unchanging self-identity of faith and its varying performance in the concrete. Only the phenomenal level is seen as subject to a historical dialectic; the essence of the Church and of faith is in effect removed from history. Then, corresponding to that fundamental presupposition, a distinction is made between practical or existential theology and speculative or essential theology, and it is taken as self-evident that practical is subordinated to speculative theology as existence follows upon essence. The same dualism also affects the part played by the social sciences in working out the problems raised in practical theology: their critical impact is restricted from the outset to the concrete performance of the Church, and they are not allowed to raise questions about its essence.

In brief, there is a cleavage between theory, concerned with essence, and practice, concerned with performance. Theory is

---

11   Franz Xaver Arnold, Karl Rahner, Viktor Schurr and Leonard M. Weber, eds., *Handbuch der Pastoraltheologie: Praktische Theologie der Kirche in ihrer Gegenwart* (Freiburg and Vienna: Herder, 1964–72).

disengaged as independent. Theory as self-sufficient dominates over practice. The essence of the Church and faith is removed from the contradictions and dialectic of history, which affect only the level of manifestation and performance.

All those characteristics, when judged by the Marxist principle of the unity of theory and practice, amount to a description of an ideology. There is no genuine mediation of faith through history.

Here it may be noted that Marx regarded what he called 'Hegel's compromise with religion', namely Hegel's re-establishment of religion after its negation in the dialectical process, as showing 'the falsehood of his whole argument', as being 'the root of Hegel's *false* positivism, or of his merely *apparent* criticism'. One of the arguments with which Marx supports his case is that 'the existent which Hegel *supersedes* in philosophy is not therefore the *actual* religion ... but religion itself as an object of knowledge, i.e. *dogmatics*'.[12] In other words, according to Marx, Hegel does not offer a genuine mediation. His vaunted reconciliation of religion and reason does not touch actual religion, does not come to grips with the real basis of religion, but remains a purely theoretical exercise. Precisely because Hegel remains within the merely theoretical, he remains within human alienation. If Hegel had moved out of theory, he would have recognized religion for what it truly is: alienated consciousness. Hegel's dialectic preserves religion because the mediation it effects is purely theoretical.

The application of that criticism to Catholic theology is not hard to see. Much post-Vatican theology, with its talk of 'the People of God', 'the Eucharistic community', and so on, floats free in the realms of mere theory without being grounded in an objective analysis of the actual reality of faith as found in practice in the Church. Far from satisfactorily countering Marx's critique of religion, it simply confirms his conclusion that religion is ideology through and through, that is, an illusion or a merely theoretical aspect of human alienated consciousness. Are the theologians prepared to imperil their

---

[12] Economic and Philosophical Manuscripts, Third Manuscript. See Bottomore, ed., *Karl Marx: Early Writings*, p. 210.

cherished theories and the believers their unchanging doctrines by accepting an indissoluble unity of theory and *praxis*?

Next for consideration would come the theologies of secularization. These theologies assert and elaborate a correspondence between the modern world and the Christian faith. Their general contention is that the distinctive character of the modern world over against the ancient and medieval worlds – that is, its secularity – far from being opposed to the Christian faith, has its origin in Christianity. I have examined the question of secularization in my book, *God's Grace in History*.[13]

According to a Marxist way of thinking, the problem of secularization is badly posed. The whole problematic supposes that human history, whether past or future, is in the first place a history of changes in the spiritual attitudes of men and women. But history is basically the history of human productive activities and the social relationships resulting from them. It is an error to think that religion was the dominant factor determining society in the past, and it is equally erroneous to suppose that the replacement of religion by some other form of theoretical thought is going to transform society in the future. For a Marxist theme of secularization, however interpreted, exaggerates the part played by religion and employs an idealist conception of history as the unfolding of consciousness. History in reality is the history of men and women bound to nature through labour.

Before concluding this brief account of the work of critical theology, I should like to add a few remarks that might help to clarify what the theologians of that standpoint are trying to do.

Fundamental for them as a consequence of their acceptance of the Marxist unity of theory and *praxis* is a conviction that the permanent self-identity of the Christian faith cannot be presupposed. History cannot be anticipated, and any such continuous self-identity has to be realized in history. They reject a theoretical system of identity. There is no purely theoretical centre of reference which can serve in an abstract, speculative way as a norm of identity. Truth does not yet exist; it cannot be reached

---

[13] London: Collins Fontana Books, 1966.

by interpretation, but it has to be produced by change. For these theologians, therefore, faith is in a strong sense mediated in history through *praxis*. *Praxis* is not the application of already known truth or the carrying out of a transhistorical ideal; it is that process in and through which one comes to know present reality and future possibilities. If faith is mediated in *praxis*, it must renounce an *a priori* claim to self-identity and universality. Not to do so is to continue with the idealists to seek salvation in a theoretical reconciliation of the contradictions of human history.

However, if the mediation of faith through *praxis* is consistently accepted, that means the destruction of theology in the current sense of the articulation of the immanent self-understanding of faith. Theology loses its boundaries as an independent discipline, because the only appropriate context for the conscious articulation of *praxis* is a theory of the development of society in its total reality. Included within such a comprehensive theory would be a critique of theological consciousness, replacing theology as a separate science. The present division of the sciences reflects the alienated state of society. While striving for the overcoming of the present division of labour, the task of theology is to function as a critique of theology. The negativity of the present critical task is inevitable because of the social situation.

My purpose here has been mainly expository, but it will be apparent that I regard the critique I have outlined as a serious challenge to theology as currently understood. However, as with the Marxist critique of religion, a merely theoretical acceptance or rejection is inappropriate. We may apply to critical theology what Wellmer says of the critical theory of society: 'the diagnosis that it offers to society, and its outline of future practice, can prove themselves ultimately only in the free acknowledgement of those individuals who have experienced as real freedom an alteration of society deriving from this theory'.[14] In other words, the diagnosis critical theology offers the Churches can be proved only by those who experience the

---

[14] Albrecht Wellmer, *Critical Theory of Society*, trans. John Cumming (New York: Herder, 1971), p. 41.

changes brought about in the Churches by it. Its appeal is to
praxis.

What, then, is required is a renewed *praxis*. But *praxis* must be
conscious as united to theory. It has been rightly noted that in
the Churches there is at present theory without practice,
practice without theory. While theology is not anchored in
practice, practice does not derive from a concrete analysis of
the actual situation, but is a bundle of unreflective expedients
promoted by the desire of the Church to survive. The *praxis* of
Christians, like all *praxis*, demands a critical analysis of present
society, intended to uncover the contradictions latent within it.
These contradictions, if Christianity is more than ideology, will
occur where Christians with their faith and hope are situated in
an objective conflict with the social order. Conscious Christian
praxis is the actualization of the conflict thus uncovered.

The question, then, is: is the good news of Christianity a
purely theoretical salvation, as Marx held, or is it a *praxis*
through which Christians participate in the dialectical process
transforming the human situation? To put it another way: is
theology the critical self-consciousness of Christian *praxis* or is
Kolakowski right when he says: 'For theology begins with the
belief that truth has already been given to us, and its intellectual effort consists not of attrition against reality but of
assimilation of something which is ready in its entirety'.[15]

The account I have just finished focuses on the meaning of
the word 'praxis' as interpreted in a Left-Hegelian and Marxist
context. However, the Marxists are by no means the only
thinkers to insist upon the priority of social practice and to
reject the intellectualism that would give pride of place and
function to contemplative or purely theoretical knowledge.

If one speaks of the primacy of the will and of the role played
in knowledge by our non-intellectual and passional nature,
Americans will at once be reminded of the pragmatism of
William James. Here, however, I want to return to the
consideration of that Catholic philosopher already dealt with
in the Introduction, namely, Maurice Blondel. His work has

---

[15] Leszek Kolakowski, *Marxism and Beyond: On Historical Understanding and Individual
Responsibility* (London: Pall Mall Press, 1968), p. 41.

been described as a supernatural pragmatism by John Milbank.[16]

There was some interaction between James and Blondel. James made a great effort to obtain a copy of *L'Action*. In the end he had to borrow Blondel's only personal copy, which he read and returned after three months. James copied out whole paragraphs from Blondel's writing. He praised him as an absolutely original thinker and cited him in two of his books. At the same time he does not show any great understanding of Blondel's distinctive theses. As for Blondel, he was briefly tempted to designate his own philosophy as pragmatism but he soon dropped the idea, because for him the pragmatist criterion of truth remained too extrinsic and utilitarian. Again, the pragmatist opposition between thought and action was foreign to Blondel's outlook.[17]

Blondel's thought is not anti-metaphysical, although in his early writings he does undervalue theoretical or propositional knowledge. At the heart of his entire work is the conviction that true knowledge is that in which the total personality, intelligence and will is committed. It is a knowledge by connaturality.[18] He distinguishes two forms of knowledge or, better, two dimensions of knowledge. His terminology varies in a somewhat confusing way. He distinguishes knowledge of phenomena and knowledge of being. In some places the distinction is made between subjective knowledge and objective knowledge. He uses those terms in an unusual fashion. Subjective knowledge is knowledge of phenomena, knowledge that precedes the affirmation of God. Objective knowledge is the knowledge of being. It flows from the affirmation of God as the Uniquely Necessary. He also makes use of Newman's distinction between real and notional knowledge though he later rejects that formulation as being too abstract. Then, again, the distinction

---

[16] John Milbank, *Theology and Social Theory: Beyond Secular Reason* (Oxford: Blackwell, 1990), pp. 249–52.

[17] James M. Somerville, 'Maurice Blondel 1861–1949', *Thought*, 36 (1961), pp. 371–2, Oliva Blanchette, 'Introduction', to Maurice Blondel, *Action (1893): Essay on a Critique of Life and the Science of Practice* (Notre Dame, IN: University of Notre Dame Press, 1984), pp. xvii–xviii.

[18] Roger Aubert, *Le Problème de L'Acte de Foi* (Louvain: Warny, 1945), p. 286.

becomes a distinction between effective and speculative knowledge. What lies behind these various formulations is the conviction that knowledge in the full sense is not just the representation of the object but possession of its being.[19]

There is no opposition between thought and action because thought is a cosmic event beyond the various states of consciousness or subconsciousness. One must seek for the origin of thought right into the physical world. Thought does not rise from nothing; it is rooted in the material universe as finding there its origin and its permanent and necessary embodiment.[20]

Blondel makes a distinction between practical science, which comes with life itself, and the science of practice, which starts with practical science but constitutes a critique of life and encompasses all that makes human action what it is from the lowest stirrings in human nature to the highest aspirations of the human spirit. Hence, Blondel proceeds to elaborate the dialectic of action, which I outlined in the Introduction. Throughout that dialectic he is led to maintain that without the supernatural any account of human action is incomplete. Through working out the implications of the dialectic, philosophy reaches a completeness or adequation, not by a correspondence between speculative thought and reality but by a correspondence between thought and life.[21]

In view of Blondel's emphasis upon the concrete embodiment of thought, one is not misinterpreting him in attributing to him the thesis that theory and practice form an indissoluble whole. This may be illustrated by his account of the act of faith. This account was one of the chief points of controversy which his work provoked. He maintained that when a person came to the threshold of faith but was held back by an inability to make the free surrender of the self to God that person should act as though believing. Practice could precede the assent of faith. Faith would come through practice.

For it is not from thought that faith passes over into the act, it is from practice that it draws down a divine light for the spirit. God acts in

[19] Henri Bouillard, *Blondel et le Christianisme* (Paris: Edition du Seuil, 1961), pp. 137ff.
[20] Jean Lacroix, *Maurice Blondel* (Paris: Presses Universitaires de France, 1963), p. 42.
[21] Blanchette, 'Introduction' (see n. 17 above), p. xvi.

this action and that is why the thought that follows the act is richer by an infinity than that which precedes it. It has entered into a new world where no philosophical speculation can lead it or follow it.[22]

Unfortunately, Blondel's thought was trivialized by those who accused him wrongly of urging a disregard of the Church's ritual rules. In fact, it is an application of the principle that runs through his writings that the knowledge of being does not precede but comes after the free choice of the human subject. The recognition that both metaphysics and supernatural faith emerge only after the options confronting human beings is what justifies us in seeing Blondel's work as an original development of the recurrent theme of the unity of theory and practice.

[22] Blondel, *Action (1893)*, p. 371.

CHAPTER 6

Revelation, historical continuity and the rationality of tradition

The purpose of this chapter is to bring the problematic of revelation into relationship with the problematic of critical theory. Revelation is considered as a distinguishing feature of the Western religions, namely Judaism, Christianity and Islam, all of Semitic or Near Eastern origin, in contrast to the Eastern or Asian religions. That means that revelation is linked to belief in a personal God. The God who reveals and is revealed is conceived as a personal agent who acts and who speaks. Revelation is, therefore, understood as a communication from a personal God to human persons as persons, that is, as beings capable of an intelligent and free response to a divine communication.

It is useful here to apply the distinction made by Gilbert Ryle between achievement verbs and task verbs.[1] Achievement verbs express success in attaining some goal; task verbs express the activities or process required to reach that goal. 'The athlete won the race' – 'win' is an achievement verb; 'The athlete ran the race' – 'run' is a task verb. We do not observe the distinction rigidly, often borrowing achievement verbs to express the process leading to the achievement. For example, we speak of a runner winning a race while still running. But it makes for clarity to be aware of the difference in logical behaviour between the two classes of verb. 'Reveal' is best understood as an achievement verb. It expresses the

---

[1] Gilbert Ryle, *The Concept of Mind* (Harmondsworth: Penguin, 1988 (first published 1949)), pp. 143–7. The application of the concept of achievement verbs to revelation was made by William J. Abraham, *Divine Revelation and the Limits of Historical Criticism* (Oxford: Oxford University Press, 1982), p. 11.

accomplishment of a communication between God and the recipient of the revelation. It affirms the completion of a communication, while allowing that the processes leading to the achieved communication may be many and various. These processes will be expressed by a variety of task verbs.

There are, therefore, two possible lines of reflection concerning revelation. The first examines the many means God has used to achieve a communication with human persons. These range from a providential ordering of events and images, so as to provoke new insights in a mind enlightened by grace, to paranormal phenomena, such as visions and miracles. The second line of reflection takes for granted the processes leading to revelation and seeks to analyse its constituent elements, asking questions about its permanence. Revelation should not be identified with the processes that bring it about, but should be understood as a relationship of communication in which God addresses human beings.

Some further qualifications are called for. Revelation as it concerns theology is public revelation, namely, revelation where the recipient is a community, even if the activities leading to revelation are the activities of representative individuals. Public revelation is achieved when an initial communication is embodied in a community and institutionalized, so that subsequent generations may join themselves to that communication, adding their response to the response of earlier generations. That means that revelation in its permanent reality is a particular kind of tradition. What distinguishes a revealed tradition as revealed?

Revelation is an interpersonal communication between God conceived as a personal agent and human beings as free and responsible subjects. As such, revelation is characterized by contingency and positivity. It is the result of a free, gratuitous intervention on the part of God. As the result of free action, both on the part of God and on the part of human beings, revelation is a contingent state of affairs. It does not arise by natural necessity; it cannot be derived logically from universal principles. All finite beings and events are contingent, but revelation is not contingent merely in that sense. It is contingent because it cannot be claimed as a necessary feature of any finite order. It remains a free gift – unexpected, uncalled for, supererogatory. That is what is meant in speaking of it as a grace or, more technically, as supernatural, that is, as out of proportion to the inherent constituents of any created nature.

For that reason the authority revelation claims is in the last analysis always positive, namely, tied to a particular occurrence and not reducible to the universal claims of a general rationality. Consequently, for revelation to be achieved, it demands faith on the part of the recipient. Faith is the response of a person to the divine intervention of communication. Revelation as an achievement includes the faith by which it is received and, as a divine gift or initiative, it includes the enlightenment of the mind of the recipient to recognize the divine communication. Revelation is the coming together of a divinely controlled objective process and a divine illumination of the mind to interpret it aright. It is essentially historical, having its origin in a particular set of events and its permanence and continuity as a particular tradition.

What is revealed? What, in other words, is the content of the revelation? Since revelation is conceived by an analogy with verbal communication, we may make use here of Roman Jakobson's distinction of the six constitutive factors in any verbal communication. An *addresser* sends a *message* to an *addressee*. To be operative the *message* must be in a *context* and expressed in a common *code*. Finally, there must be some connection or *contact* between the *addresser* and *addressee*, enabling them to enter and remain in communication. Notice that meaning is not limited to the *message*, but belongs to the totality of the verbal communication with its six constituent factors.[2]

Those who identify revelation as inner experience are highlighting the factor *contact*, but at the expense of the other

---

[2] For two texts from Jakobson's voluminous writings, see David Lodge, ed., *Modern Criticism and Theory: A Reader* (London and New York: Longman, 1988), pp. 32–57.

factors. Revelation always includes an experiential component, but it is not complete until the experience has been articulated in a *message*.

What, then, is the *message*? Those who reject the propositional view of revelation, namely, the concept of revelation as a set of doctrines, formulated in propositions and transmitted as an unalterable deposit of truth, are right to the extent that revelation does not belong to the realm of theory. The *message* of revelation is a *praxis*, an ethical life, a way of being and acting. It may be partially articulated in propositions. It may stimulate theoretical reflection. But it is essentially the establishment of a practical way of life.

The concept of the *message* in revelation helps us to understand what can serve as a common *code* in a divine communication. The language used will not be the expression of univocal concepts. Both concepts and language will proceed by the use of analogy; in other words, by exploiting the resemblances between revealed content and the ordinary objects of human intelligence, while denying identity. Such analogical grouping, with the figurative language that goes with it, does not provide a suitable basis for the erection of theoretical systems. The theoretical reflection to which it gives rise must remain tentative and very much a function of the secular intellectual *context* in which revelation is operative. The centre of reference which gives a revealed tradition its identity and continuity is the *praxis* it embodies. Revelation is basically a way of life. The Word of God is not just a series of statements asserting propositional truths. It is a word of command, of promise, of forgiveness, of condemnation, of persuasion. There are indeed those Christians who insist on understanding revelation as the transmission of a set of doctrines, and that doctrinalization of the Christian faith has led to a one-sided stress upon orthodoxy as the preservation of doctrinal purity. However, the emergence of the various liberation theologies has led to the recognition of the primacy of *praxis* in relation to religious faith, granted that *praxis* includes an intellectual component.

In sum, public revelation is an achieved communication

between God conceived as a personal agent and a community
of human beings. Once achieved in the foundation of a
community, the communication is rendered permanent in a
tradition. What is communicated is a way of life, together
with the insight it presupposes into the human condition and
God's saving relationship with men and women. Because
revelation, as understood by Christians, Jews and Muslims,
is a contingent divine intervention, not explicable as a result
of human intelligence and action, it invites human beings
into mystery. In other words, it leads them into a mode
of life, with an accompanying set of beliefs, disproportionate
to what is implied in human agency and human intelligence
as human. Hence, revelation is seen as a free gift of God,
a grace supernaturally bestowed upon those whom God
chooses.

There are two lines of thought where discussion among
critical theorists has a bearing upon the understanding of
revelation. The two themes are continuity and rationality. A
revealed religion makes a strong claim to continuity. It does so
because of the account of the past it must give and its vision of
the future. The account of the past has to include a story of an
initial communication from which its particular tradition took
its rise and which remains as its permanent basis. Again, its
vision of the future looks forward to a new state of affairs,
individual, collective or both, which as the final destiny of
humankind will alone replace the religious tradition in its
present functioning.

Thus, the Christian religion claims immutability for itself as
the final revelation. The revelation achieved in Jesus Christ is
regarded as closed with the death of the last apostle; nothing
further can be added. Hence the criterion of Christian truth
given in these words of Vincent of Lerins: 'quod ubique, quod
semper, quod ab omnibus' (what is taught everywhere, always
and by all). Novelty is heresy. However, the rise of historical
scholarship has made it impossible to ignore the all-pervasiveness of change. So, since the nineteenth century the question of
the identity in change of the Christian revelation has been a
theological problem. Newman suggested 'development' as an

alternative to immutability on the one hand and to corruption or loss of identity on the other. But while Newman pointed to the fact of development, he did not have any theory of development to offer. He simply argued that in the midst of a development affecting all forms of Christianity the Roman Catholic Church was the least unlike the primitive Church.[3] One cannot say that theologians since have come up with a theory that in a satisfactory fashion explains the strict continuity or identity claimed by the Christian tradition. We need, then, to widen the question by considering the general problem of historical continuity.

Baumgartner in his *Kontinuität und Geschichte*[4] argues that historical continuity is given with the narrative construction of historical knowledge, that continuity belongs to the narrative structure as one of its properties. It does not depict or reproduce a previously existing temporal duration of some subject. Historical continuity is not to be identified with temporal duration. It is an autonomous construction, not derived from a prior temporal structure, but the result of the form-giving constructivity, characteristic of historical consciousness.

Historical consciousness, Baumgartner continues, is first constituted in the medium of a story. The idea of a story is a far better starting point for reconstructing historical knowledge than *Verstehen* or hermeneutic understanding. The narrative structure of a story gathers together the three essential features of historical knowledge: retrospectivity, constructivity and practical interest. *History is a retrospective construction, motivated by a need for communication and directed by a practical intent.*

Here Baumgartner rejoins themes from Habermas. In his turn Habermas has commented briefly on Baumgartner's

3 Cf. Nicholas Lash, *Newman on Development: The Search for an Explanation in History* (Shepherdstown: Patmos, 1975), and his summary account in Alan Richardson and John Bowden, eds., *The Westminster Dictionary of Christian Theology* (Philadelphia: Westminster, 1983), s.v. 'Development, Doctrinal'.

4 Hans Michael Baumgartner, *Kontinuität und Geschichte: Zur Kritik und Metakritik der historischen Vernunft* (Frankfurt am Main: Suhrkamp Verlag, 1972).

concept of historical continuity.[5] Both Habermas and Baumgartner make extensive use of Danto's analysis of historical knowledge. Though each has his own reservations to make about Danto's treatment, both draw heavily upon Danto in setting forth the structure of historical knowledge. Let me give, then, the points of agreement before discussing their differences.

First, we cannot conceive of history without organizational schemes. These schemes are always linked to particular human interests. History differs from science, not in using organizational schemes, but in the kind of scheme it uses. History organizes events into stories.

Second, history is all of a piece. There is no way in which we can distinguish pure description from interpretation or plain from significant narrative. To do history at all is to go beyond what is given. The production of a narrative organization inevitably involves us in a subjective factor. There is, Danto remarks, an element of sheer arbitrariness in the narrative organization of events, which is always done in relation to the topical interest of some human being or other.

Third, the idea of a complete description of an event is logically impossible. To describe an event completely is to locate it in all the right stories. We can never do this, because to use the striking phrase of Danto, 'we are temporally provincial with regard to the future'.[6] A complete description of an event is impossible for the same reason as the speculative philosophy

5 Cf. Baumgartner, *Kontinuität und Geschichte*, pp. 269–94; Habermas's comments upon Danto are given in two places: (1) *Zur Logik der Sozialwissenschaften* (Frankfurt am Main: Suhrkamp Verlag, 1970), pp. 267–74, this section has been translated in Jürgen Habermas, 'A review of Gadamer's *Truth and Method*', in *Understanding and Social Inquiry*, ed. Fred R. Dallmayr and Thomas A. McCarthy, (Notre Dame, IN: University of Notre Dame Press, 1977), pp. 346–50; (2) 'Geschichte und Evolution', in Jürgen Habermas, *Zur Rekonstruktion des historischen Materialismus* (Frankfurt am Main: Suhrkamp Verlag, 1976), pp. 204–7, this essay has been translated as 'History and evolution', in *Telos*, 39 (1979), pp. 5–44, the pages on Danto being 8–11.
6 Arthur C. Danto, *Analytical Philosophy of History* (Cambridge: Cambridge University Press, 1968), p. 142.

of history: we do not know the future and therefore we cannot relate events to it.

Fourth, history is necessarily retrospective. Narrative statements can deal only with past events. Danto gives an analysis of the structure of narrative sentences, which is accepted by Habermas and Baumgartner. Narrative sentences refer to at least two time-separated events, though they only describe (are only about) the earliest event to which they refer. Thus, a narrative sentence describes an event E_1 in relation to an event E_2. E_2 is always later than E_1, although it is past for the historian. Even when the standpoint of the historian is his own contemporary situation, his description of E_1 must be related to the already determined features of that situation or, in other words, to the past present. To relate E_1 to a future event, an event not yet determined and in that sense past, is to write a futuristic novel not history.

In brief, Baumgartner and Habermas agree with Danto that history is a retrospective narrative organization of events, and so far the analysis of narrative has clarified the constructivity and retrospectivity of historical consciousness and knowledge. But there is a third feature of historical consciousness, which has been previously mentioned: the practical interest or intent of the historian, guiding his choice of a frame of interpretation.

On the latter point, Habermas objects to Danto's contention that the function of the topical interest of the historian, necessary as it is, introduces an element of sheer arbitrariness. The procedure would be arbitrary only if we suppose a complete description is a meaningful historical idea. It is not; it cannot be consistently formulated. Even the last historian in time would view events from a standpoint not acquired from the events themselves, and as soon as the historian acts at all, he produces new relationships, which will combine into a new story from a fresh standpoint. Hence 'complete description' ascribes to history a claim to a theoretical contemplation of historical reality, a claim which is illegitimate and cannot be redeemed.

But that does not make history arbitrary. The historian does not organize his knowledge according to pure theory, but within the framework of his own life-practice. His choice of a frame of interpretation, guided by a practical interest, is dependent upon his expectations of future events. Thus, the historian does anticipate the future, but his anticipations are not part of the narrated history. History itself remains retrospective. The anticipations of the future, rooted in a practical interest, are not arbitrary. The historian from the viewpoint of practice anticipates end-states, and thereby events in their multiplicity coalesce into action-orientating stories. *History is not an imitation or duplication of the past, but a construction of past events in relation to practice and to the horizon of future expectations, which forms the context of practice.*

Baumgartner on his part objects to Danto's understanding of continuity. Danto recognizes the constructive function of narrative organization in forming particular temporal structures out of the total happenings of a stretch of time. To that extent he conceives historical continuity as a product of narrative organization. But Danto qualifies his view by arguing that change requires some continuous identity in the subject of change, and that it is an implicit reference to a continuous subject that gives unity to a historical narrative. Baumgartner does not agree. Historical continuity may presuppose or include a temporally enduring person, event or element, but such temporal duration of a subject or element offers the possibility not the actuality of history. The identity of an individual, say Napoleon, through the temporal duration of his life belongs to the substratum of his history. It is not yet the historical continuity produced by the narrative construction of his biography. Further, the case of an individual subject is not a good analogy for understanding the historical continuity of such historical structures as the French Revolution or the Middle Ages. Baumgartner, therefore, insists that historical continuity is a property of narrative construction. History creates it; history does not reproduce a prior continuity of events.

Habermas, however, finds Baumgartner here guilty of an oversight in failing to consider 'that narratives not only organize the stories that the historian tells but also those that the historian presupposes as stories: the historian finds a pre-constituted, in fact narratively pre-constituted field of objects'.[7] Habermas admits that in a certain sense historical continuity is first constituted by the narrative of the historian. But this continuity is based 'on the unifying force of the vital contexts in which the events acquired their relevance for participants before the historian comes along'.[8] He finds the model for this pre-given unity in the identity of the self and the unity of its life-history kept through a series of narrative constructions. History is an objective life-context. It is not constructed 'theoretically' for the first time by the historian. The constructions of the historian follow upon and are added to the already formed traditional constructions.[9]

There is no denial, then, by Habermas that historical continuity is a matter of narrative construction. But he distinguishes two levels of narrative. There are the narratives produced by participants in the course of their life-practice, and there are the narratives produced subsequently by the historian, who chooses an interpretative frame, and thus decides on the beginning and end of a history and on which events are to be regarded as relevant. First-level or participant narrative would seem in this analysis to be an essential form for human action and self-understanding. However, Habermas's own reflections dwell more upon the second level, and, in particular, upon its relation to theory.

In discussing the use of theories within history, Habermas distinguishes historical research and history writing. The role of historical research is instrumental, and part of the knowledge it makes available to the historian for his descriptions are various theories. History writing is descriptive, and must in principle retain a narrative form. A historian may apply theories to history, but he remains a historian only as long as he applies them within the framework of a narrative. Unlike the participant narrator, the historian does theoretically expand the common-sense basis of narrative explanation, but the historian does so without abandoning the narrative structure. 'If he did

---

[7] 'History and evolution', p. 10 n. 9.   [8] *Ibid.*, pp. 9–10.
[9] Cf. *ibid.*, p. 10 n. 9.

abandon the narrative frame of reference, the historian would have to give up his role as history writer.'[10]

With the life-world as its context, historical narrative has an ineluctable relation to practice. In it actions and events are explained with reference to norms and values, intentions and motives.[11] Here Habermas's account coincides with Alasdair MacIntyre's as given in 'Epistemological crises, dramatic narrative, and the philosophy of science'.[12] For MacIntyre, narrative is always moral narrative, for 'narrative requires an evaluative framework in which good or bad character helps to produce unfortunate or happy outcomes'.[13] Dramatic narrative, he goes on to argue, 'is the crucial form for the understanding of human action'.[14] So much so, indeed, that the natural sciences and *a fortiori* the social sciences as rational forms of enquiry are dependent upon the rationality of historical reason and the dramatic narratives it originates.

MacIntyre thus gives narrative so fundamental a role that he makes the rationality of the sciences, both natural and social, dependent upon the rationality of historical reason and its narratives.

To understand that surprising contention, we need to refer to MacIntyre's concept of an epistemological crisis. An epistemological crisis is when an accustomed way for relating *seems* and *is* breaks down. What has been taken as evidence pointing unambiguously in one direction turns out to be equally susceptible to rival interpretations. To share a culture is to share schemata that are both constitutive and normative for intelligible action by myself and at the same time are means for

---

[10] *Ibid.*, p. 7.   [11] Cf. *ibid.*, pp. 8–9.

[12] First published in *The Monist*, 60 (1977), pp. 453–71; reprinted in Gary Gutting, ed., *Paradigms and Revolutions: Appraisals and Applications of Thomas Kuhn's Philosophy of Science* (Notre Dame, IN, and London: University of Notre Dame Press, 1980), pp. 54–74. The quotations are from the latter. For the further development of MacIntyre's thought in relation to the nature of moral enquiry see his three books: *After Virtue: The Study in Moral Theory* (Notre Dame, IN: University of Notre Dame Press, 1981); *Whose Justice? Which Rationality?* (Notre Dame, IN: University of Notre Dame Press, 1988); *Three Rival Versions of Moral Inquiry* (London: Duckworth, 1990).

[13] 'Epistemological crises', in *Paradigms*, p. 57.   [14] *Ibid.*, p. 66.

interpreting the actions of others. In an epistemological crisis an individual is brought 'to recognize the possibility of systematically different possibilities of interpretation, of the existence of alternative and rival schemata which yield mutually incompatible accounts of what is going on around him'.[15] Such an epistemological crisis can affect ordinary agents or take place within science or philosophy. The crisis is resolved by the construction of a new narrative. At the level of the ordinary agent, the new narrative 'enables the agent to understand *both* how he or she could intelligibly have held his or her original beliefs *and* how he or she could have been so drastically misled by them'. At the scientific level, the new narrative reconstructs the scientific tradition when it is thrown into crisis by new theory.

The criterion of a successful theory is that it enables us to understand its predecessors in a newly intelligible way. It, at one and the same time, enables us to understand precisely why its predecessors have to be rejected or modified and also why, without and before its illumination, past theory could have remained credible. It introduces new standards for evaluating the past. It recasts the narrative which constitutes reconstruction of the scientific tradition.[16]

It is because of the possibility of constructing an intelligible narrative, relating theories as successive episodes in the history of science, that we compare theories with one another and give an account of why one theory is superior to another.

It is more rational to accept one theory or paradigm and to reject its predecessor when the later theory or paradigm provides a stand-point from which the acceptance, the life-story, and the rejection of the previous theory or paradigm can be recounted in more intelligible historical narrative than previously. An understanding of the concept of the superiority of one physical theory to another requires a prior understanding of the concept of the superiority of one historical narrative to another. The theory of scientific rationality has to be embedded in a philosophy of history.[17]

That is why scientific reason is dependent upon historical reason.

[15] *Ibid.*, p. 55.   [16] *Ibid.*, p. 62.   [17] *Ibid.*, p. 70.

In the course of his argument, MacIntyre develops the concept of tradition. Tradition is constituted by a conflict of interpretations of the tradition itself. It embodies the narrative of an argument. Constantly threatened by the danger of lapsing into incoherence, it is rescued by an argumentative reconstruction of its narrative. At certain periods traditions need revolutionary reconstitution for their continuance. Far from excluding conflict, tradition presupposes the omnipresence of conflict, both within each tradition and between traditions, and the conflict itself has a history susceptible to rival interpretations. To belong to a tradition is to enter into an argument and to make the continuous argument intelligible by narrative.

What bearing has the discussion just outlined upon the concept of revelation? It may well lead us to consider that revelation is best conceived as a historical narrative constructed from within a practical way of life.

History, it has been argued, is a retrospective narrative organization of events. Further, that construction of past events has been seen as done in relation to practice and under a vision of the future. Two levels of narrative have been distinguished: narratives produced from within life-practice and narratives constructed subsequently by the historian.

All that may be said of revelation. Revelation is a narrative of past events, organized from within a way of life and understood as a divinely communicated pattern of events, serving to ground that way of life. Revelation itself is first-level narrative: theology offers a second-level narrative. In history as revelation, as distinct from profane history, the vision of the future has a more prominent function. Hope is central to a religious way of life. It is true that hope does not remove our ignorance of the future; it is not knowledge of future events. Hence future events are not incorporated into our narrative. Nevertheless, eschatological expectations form a symbolic epilogue to the revealed narrative, assuring us that despite the limited scope of the narratives we live by, there is final meaning.

Revelation, history, tradition: all are marked by positivity, because the claim they make upon our assent is bound up with their particularity. But can a claim rooted in a particular history, a particular set of events, a particular tradition, justify itself as rational? Is not reason essentially universal, so that an appeal to reason is an appeal to universal principles, to universal criteria and arguments? An appeal to a particular historical construction or to a particular tradition cannot be other, it would seem, than an appeal to authority. If that is in fact the case, then when confronted with the plurality of traditions we have no defence against the relativist contention that no issue between conflicting traditions is rationally decidable.

Alasdair MacIntyre[18] argues that the relativist challenge can be met by recognizing the special kind of rationality proper to traditions. That rationality consists in an openness to development. Every tradition begins in a condition of pure historical contingency in which beliefs, institutions and practices constitute a given to be taken as authoritative without questioning. The first unquestioning stage comes to an end when new situations giving rise to new questions lead to alternative and incompatible interpretations. The crisis is resolved by the construction of a new narrative. The new narrative allows the agent to understand both how he or she could have held his or her original beliefs and how he or she was misled by them, so as to come to need new formulations and new evaluations. The tradition avoids repudiation and remains worthy of rational assent as long as it can find within itself resources to meet new situations and questions with sufficient inventiveness for the reformulation and re-evaluation of its authoritative texts and beliefs.

Nothing characterizes the Christian tradition better than to describe it as a conflict of interpretations. Referring to the fact that from the beginning the Christian Church contained often contradictory movements within itself, the historian Frend remarks: 'It is difficult to point to any time after the Ascension

---

[18] Alasdair MacIntyre, *Whose Justice? Which Rationality?* (Notre Dame, IN: University of Notre Dame Press, 1988), especially Chapter XVIII: 'The rationality of traditions', pp. 349–69.

when it was truly one'.[19] Down through the centuries the Church has been constituted by followers of Christ locked together in argument over their beliefs and practices. What the Christian tradition embodies is the narrative of an argument. It has constantly been threatened with dissolution and saved by the reconstruction of its narrative – a retelling that incorporates new insights or even revolutionary changes of interpretation. Orthodoxy may be conceived as the continuously reconstructed narrative. It is, however, the narrative of an argument. The attempt to make it a body of unchanging interpretations to be accepted without question is to block its transmission into new historical and cultural situations and eventually to kill it. All belong to the tradition who are willing to enter into the argument. Those who refuse the argument that continually reconstitutes the tradition put themselves outside the tradition, as the flat-earthers have put themselves outside the scientific tradition. On the other hand, groups outside the mainstream who are still arguing represent elements that have not yet been adequately accounted for in the present narrative of the tradition and are rightly calling for a further reconstruction of the narrative and its argument.

The continuity of the Christian tradition is, therefore, achieved by narrative. But here I agree with Habermas against Baumgartner that what constitutes the basic continuity is not the narrative of the historian, but the narrative that originates in the life-world as its connatural expression. The Church lives as a community in the unity of its life by constantly retelling its story. All the same, while the narrative of the historian presupposes and expands the first-level participant narrative, historiography, however rigorous its methods, does retain an indispensable practical function in relation to the life of the community. Even the history of the historian has a particular perspective on the past, derived from the situation of the historian, and has a practical mission in relation to the future. The practical function of the historian *vis-à-vis* the community is especially evident at times of crisis – and crises punctuate the

19 W. H. C. Frend, *The Early Church From the Beginnings to 461* (London: SCM Press Ltd., 1982), p. 1.

ongoing life of any major tradition. The resources available to the historian are called upon in the task of reconstructing the narrative, so as to rescue continuity in the midst of revolutionary change. As an example, one might cite the rewriting of the history of Reformation by Catholic historians in recent decades. The gradual growth of the ecumenical movement made unviable the previous account of Protestantism. It became necessary to retell the story so as to combine a positive appreciation of the Protestant Reformation with a continued adherence to Catholic values. The historian, then, remains tied to the life-world of the community by his or her historico-hermeneutical situation and practical mission. That, however, does not exclude the historian from making use of available theories in historical research – indeed, it would seem to require him or her to do so. But it is through narrative that the unity and continuity of tradition are preserved in the context of an unavoidable conflict of interpretations.

CHAPTER 7

The political use and misuse of religious language

Spending a sabbatical leave in Israel, I could not avoid being confronted with the claim of some religious Israelis that God had given them the Holy Land in perpetuity. They had, so they argued, a God-given right that justified them in dismissing the claims of any others, notably the Palestinians, who had come to occupy Eretz Yisrael in the course of history. Any merely human right, founded in international law, had to yield to the divine right of the Jews, founded in God's covenant and promise. 'God gave us this land' – a sentence that would seem to come spontaneously to the lips of even some secular Israelis when challenged, say, about Israel's policy over the West Bank and Gaza. As Menachem Begin said: 'Nobody has the right to tell me whether I can stay in Judea and Samaria, since this right is given to me by God the Father of Abraham, Isaac and Jacob'.[1]

The Jewish claim to the Holy Land on the basis of God's gift is accepted by some Christians as well as by the Jews themselves. It would be difficult to find a stronger statement than that of Jacques Maritain in the Post-Scriptum (1964) to his *Le Mystère d'Israel et autres essais*.[2] There he insisted that it is absolutely, divinely certain that Israel has the incontestable right to the Land of Canaan. The people of Israel, he asserted, is the only people in the world to whom a land, the Land of Canaan, was given by the one transcendent God, creator of the universe and of the human race, and what God has given is

---

[1] Quoted without reference by Gabriel Habib in Koson Srisang, ed., *Perspectives on Political Ethics: An Ecumenical Enquiry* (Geneva: WCC Publications, 1983), p. 121.

[2] (Paris: Desclée de Brouwer, 1965), pp. 243–5.

given forever. Maritain went on to declare that the fact of this gift of the Land is a matter of faith for Christians as well as for Jews, because the Christian faith acknowledges the Holy Spirit is the principal author of Scripture, where the gift of the Land to the people of Israel is affirmed.

I am sure there must be others beside myself whose first, spontaneous reaction is to resist any such attempt to establish a political claim on the basis of an overriding religious right, but is that first reaction sound? No doubt what in part prompts it is a reasonable fear of introducing the absoluteness of religious faith into the realm of politics – a realm of negotiated compromise and practical agreements in a context of persistent ideological conflict. Violence would seem to be the only policy left, if politico-religious claims held as absolutes clash. However, can we keep religion out of politics? Should we even want to do so? Are we to impose Western liberalism, with the secularization of society and culture, upon other societies and cultures? Is the only acceptable political order a secular one? Are the only acceptable ideologies for social and political behaviour those that exclude or ignore religious faith?

There are other examples, besides that of the Israelis, of political claims grounded upon religious faith. Traditional Muslim teaching divided the world into *dar al-Islam*, the abode of Islam, and *dar al-harb* the abode of war. The first, besides the Islamic communities, included those non-Islamic communities that had accepted Muslim rule. All other communities and territories were the abode of war. This division was to remain valid until the definitive transformation of *dar al-harb* into *dar al-Islam* by *jihad*. The *jihad* in Islam did not consist only in fighting, but also in the non-violent propagation of faith. All the same, we are confronted with a political claim of universal scope, based not upon reciprocal agreement but upon the Islamic faith in the sovereign will of God. It is paralleled by the right claimed by medieval Christendom to subjugate both the pagans and Islam. The political claims of the Christian Church reached their apogee in the extreme version of the papal claims. Under Boniface VIII the papacy claimed universal and supreme political power in the name of Christ. The Jewish claim to the Holy Land as a divine right is only one instance of a recurrent practice of trying to ground a particular political claim upon a religious belief. Can we refuse all such politico-religious claims without falling into an irreligious and doctrinaire secularism?

It will be my contention in what follows that any attempt to ground upon religious faith a particular political claim as absolute or unalterable is invalid as a misuse of religious language. It is a misuse because it does not respect the way religious language is created and functions. The religious use of language presupposes its non-religious use. The language of transcendence rests upon the language of immanence.

But first a word of clarification. The analysis which follows is not intended as a historical account of the origin and development of religious language. The aim is to uncover the various semantic elements in metaphorical language. Historically, what came first was neither the literal sense nor the various metaphorical uses, but an undifferentiated meaning corresponding to an undifferentiated experience, which did not, for example, distinguish between politics and religion. Only gradually was the literal sense separated out from the exuberant multiplicity of metaphorical meanings. Nevertheless, despite the submergence of the literal sense in a forest of meanings, a basis of literal meaning, rooted in common human experience, is always presupposed to any set of religious images, concepts and metaphors. To put it in this way: a particular form of religious language with its particular tapestry of images always presupposes a particular social and cultural situation. There is an interaction in both directions: from the political, social and cultural context to the contemporary religious expression and from the particular form of religious expression to the contemporary political, social and cultural situation. David Nicholls in his *Deity and Domination*[3] has shown in some detail how images of God and images of the State are interrelated in the nineteenth and twentieth centuries.

[3] David Nicholls, *Deity and Domination: Images of God and the State in the Nineteenth and Twentieth Centuries* (London and New York: Routledge, 1989).

It is both instructive and fascinating to follow in an account such as that of Nicholls changes in religious language brought about by changes in political culture and changes in political culture brought about by changes in religious sensibility. But prior to a historical analysis of that kind, there is a deeper philosophico-theological question. Nicholls himself recognizes this when he remarks about his book: 'surely a necessary preliminary to this is an exhaustive consideration of whether and, if so, how we can speak about God at all'.[4] That is precisely the concern of this chapter: how can we speak of God in the various forms of human language? My contention will be that there is no specifically religious language. Further, the indirect nature of all religious meaning makes it impossible to ground a political claim upon it in confrontation with other competing claims.

To avoid losing ourselves in abstractions, let us begin by taking a very simple instance of religious language to see how the linguistic process works when it articulates religious faith.

'God is our Father'; 'I believe in God, the Father almighty.' From where do we draw the content of meaning in these and equivalent statements? Where do we find the words, images and concepts that articulate that meaning? In short, what gives us our notion of fatherhood? It comes to us from our experience of the reality of human fatherhood in its social and cultural context. The particular meaning given to fatherhood is formed by human action and interaction in their bodily, historical and institutional finite reality. Although we apply the concept and language of fatherhood to God, there is no properly or specifically religious content of meaning. The entire positive complex of meaning we use religiously when we speak of God as 'Father' is taken from our experience and knowledge of human fathers in a particular social and cultural setting. We extract the elements we wish to use, and by analogy or extrapolation we apply those elements of meaning to God. There is no such thing as a proper concept of divine fatherhood, because we have no proper knowledge at all of God. God is not a known object but a transcendent reality beyond our apprehension. The transcendence of God makes literal propositions about a divine content of meaning impossible.

Suppose, therefore, there were a debate among psychologists or sociologists concerning what the normative concept of fatherhood should be at the present stage of human development – in other words, the kind of debate that would have to deal with the feminist critique of the traditional understanding of the man–woman relationship. It would be illegitimate to appeal to the religious understanding of God to decide the issue. Why? Because language about the fatherhood of God is derived from a particular social and cultural situation. Its meaning depends upon and is drawn from that cultural context. As symbolic usage, religious language about God as 'Father' is the product of a process of extrapolation. We are dealing, then, with a dependent and derivative use of language. An improved, purified, more developed understanding of fatherhood on the immanent human level will enable us to purify, correct and improve our understanding of God. Further, one can speak of a religious critique of the existing concept of father, in so far as the experience of transcendence frees us from false absolutes and opens our minds and hearts to the full range of reality and values, thus making us sensitive to the downgrading of the feminine. One cannot, however, speak of religion as providing us through a supposed verbal revelation with data unknown beforehand to human experience and meanings unformed by human culture. Religious faith may undermine patriarchy by rejecting as idolatrous any claim it makes to be a divinely given ordinance; it is not, however, the function of religious faith to provide the positive elements required for a new, post-patriarchal social order. These have to be produced by human social and cultural creativity.

To sum up these remarks on the fatherhood of God as an example of the functioning of religious language: the religious use of the theme of fatherhood presupposes the content of meaning formed by bodily, historical and institutional experience. There is no ideational content other than that found in human practice and thought. Any development, purification or modification of the concept of fatherhood has to be done first on the level of human action and interaction. The religious use of fatherhood does not provide one with elements of meaning not found in human society and culture. There is no revealed concept of fatherhood in the sense of some new meaning and coming down from on high. What one does religiously is to select elements from the cultural inheritance and transfer these as predicates of God, indicating in some way their metaphorical or analogical usage.

We can now move from the particular example and generalize the point that there is no specifically religious content of meaning in the words, images and concepts we use in religious language. All the positive elements of meaning are taken from our experience and knowledge of finite reality, and are transferred by extrapolation and analogy to our response to transcendent reality. There must be a process of transference or shift to metaphor because God is not a known object. God is the unknown reality that stands at the term of our orientation, our spiritual thrust, towards transcendent truth and goodness. Because God remains mystery, the fundamental experience of the Transcendent is negative in the sense of an absence of formulable meaning. The positive elements of meaning are deabsolutized and rendered dispensable.

We can put the same point in another way by saying that in religious language there is always a double level of meaning and reference.[5] Because language used religiously is always as regards its ideational content taken from the world of finite objects, namely, the world of our immanent experience, its immediate meaning and reference are always in relation to that world. The language becomes religious when its immediate secular meaning and reference are cancelled or rendered inoperative by some device that compels one to interpret it as having a deeper meaning and pointing towards mystery. Various devices are used in shifting language from its immediate functioning in the world of immanent experience to a

5 For further details, see my book, *What is Living, What is Dead in Christianity Today?* (San Francisco: Harper & Row, 1986), especially Chapter 1: 'The structure of the religious imagination', pp. 7–12.

symbolic function in relation to transcendence. Ricoeur, for example, has pointed to the use of extravagance and intensification in the parables and proverbs of gospel.[6] No society, for example, could organize its economy on the basis of the parable of the labourers in the vineyard. The extravagant attitude of the owner of the vineyard indicates to us that the concern is not with the economic order but with the order of God's grace. Ian Ramsey, in his analysis of religious language, has pointed to the role of qualifiers.[7] So, we speak of 'our Heavenly Father', 'the Father almighty', 'our all-powerful, all-loving Father'. But, whatever the device used, in some way or other, the literal meaning with its reference to this world is cancelled as literal; at the same time it is saved as a metaphor referring to transcendent reality.

Religion, we say, does not or should not stand apart on its own from our secular lives as a distinct realm of thought and action. There is no proper or specific religious language precisely because religion is not a specifically distinct realm of meaning or culture. It is the opening out of every sector of human action and culture to the Unlimited, the Beyond, the Transcendent. Religious faith thus pervades the content of all the different areas of meaning and culture. It penetrates and transforms the entirety of human thought and action, bringing about a transvaluation of all values. However, it does that, not by creating new, specifically religious elements of meaning – new concepts, new actions, new rules, new words, new images – but by linking every area of human life to the experience of finitude in an openness to the Infinite. Religious language is a borrowed language. It is not literal language, but metaphorical. How, then, can it ground a particular claim? May we base a literal claim upon a metaphor? In using language religiously, we take elements of literal meaning as created by human culture and change them into metaphors of God. We may not move the other way and translate religious metaphors into literal propositions and norms. We may take human father-

---

[6]   Paul Ricoeur, 'Biblical hermeneutics', *Semeia*, 4 (1975), pp. 107–28.
[7]   Ian I. Ramsey, *Religious Language: An Empirical Placing of Theological Phrases* (New York: Macmillan, 1963), pp. 55–102.

hood and turn it into a metaphor for our understanding of God. We may not take divine fatherhood and use it as a basis for the literal subordination of women to men. Similarly, we may take political language in its literal use – for example, the language of kingship – and translate it into a metaphor of God's action. We may not, however, take the religious metaphor of kingship and use it to make an absolute claim to political power in the literal sense, as the popes did in their appeal to the kingship of Christ.

This brings us back to our starting point, namely, the attempt to base political claims upon religious belief. From what I have said, there should be no difficulty about the religious use of political language. Every area of human culture, including politics, can be used to mediate religious thought and practice. What is problematic is not the religious use of political language but the political use of religious language. If religion is to be allowed an influence in the political order, some political use of religious language must be acknowledged as legitimate. But where is the dividing line between the legitimate and illegitimate use of religious language in politics? An outstanding example of the religious use of political language is the biblical history of Israel. The Bible is indeed a monument of the translation of politics into religion. Political concepts, words and images are used to create a particular religious language. Political events are interpreted as actions of God, symbols of the divine presence and intervention. Exodus, covenant, conquest, judges, kingship: all this is originally political language. Each expression has a definite political meaning that can be studied in the culture of which Israel was a part. The political experience of Israel and the culturally conditioned language in which it was expressed were used by the religious leaders of Israel and by the biblical writers as a vehicle to mediate Israel's relationship with God.

On the level of ordinary political experience, a crowd of slaves escaped from Egypt under the leadership of Moses, established a covenantal relationship among various related tribes, and as nomads gradually conquered and settled in the land of Canaan, giving rise to a monarchy, experiencing a temporary moment of power and glory and then a longer period of subordination to the great empires, eventually meeting with political disaster and dispersion. That political experience was interpreted religiously and made a mediation of the transcendence of God by giving the political language a higher level of meaning and reference, in the manner I have sketched theoretically.

Thus, 'covenant', which originally designated a particular kind of political association, was elevated to receive a religious meaning. It was an apt expression of the unity of Israel as that had been forged in history, not as a community of blood or of land or of language or of a centralized government but, none the less, as a People, interpreted religiously as the People of God, established and guaranteed in a covenantal relationship with Yahweh that determined every aspect of Israel's life.

In principle there would seem to be nothing questionable about drawing upon the stock of political concepts, images and words to express religious faith. Nor, since all that is finite leads to God, should we question the interpretation of political events as signs of God's action. However, as the Israelite example and later the example both of Christianity and Islam show, the religious use of politics for religious purposes leads inevitably to the political use of religion for political purposes. Religious language is not created in contemplative isolation but in a context of practice. When religious people and institutions choose preferably political metaphors to express their religious faith, it is, we may reasonably presume, because their faith is an active element in the political realm. They express their religious faith in political terms because they are endeavouring to insert it as a factor into the political order. Liberation theologians, for example, prefer the political language of the Bible – the language of exodus, covenant, liberation – to the cosmological imagery of God as Creator and Sustainer of the universe, because they want religious faith to be engaged in the struggle for a just social order. But what are the principles and limits of the political involvement of religion?

The relation of religion and politics is a wide-ranging and

long-standing problem which cannot be dealt with adequately by a few brief remarks. However, I am approaching the problem from a limited standpoint. I am asking how we can exclude absolute political claims made in the name of religion – a practice that would seem to leave no solution to clashes except violence – without making secularism the only option.

We can best conceive of politics as the search and struggle for order in human existence. Human existence is understood here as inseparably both individual and social. Human beings, both individually and socially, are in pursuit of the Good – to adopt Plato's approach[8] and some kind of experience of the Good is the source of order in human life. Each society or social order has an internal dimension of meaningfulness. That meaningfulness resides in individual human beings, though not as an individual possession or achievement. It is only in and through society that human beings interpret human existence for themselves and become persons.[9]

Societies differ in the solutions they elaborate to the problem of order. They embody and articulate the source of order and the meaningfulness of human existence in a variety of ways. Since human experience is always bodily, historical and institutional, the differing embodiments imply a differing experience of the Good as the source of order. For example, to cite a well-known instance, the societies of the Ancient Near East were organized on the basis of cosmic myth. Their experience of order was cosmological. Human society was a microcosm, and human life was integrated into the cosmic order.

From our present standpoint we can ignore the detailed variety of myth, symbol and ideology used to organize society and to express its internal meaningfulness as a form of human existence. For our purpose it is enough to focus upon a broad threefold classification into sacral, secular and pluralist societies, with a subdivision of sacral societies into traditionally sacral and reactively sacral. The chief point I want to establish

---

[8] For an elaboration of Plato's treatment of the problem of order in society, see Eric Voegelin, *Order and History*, vol. 3: *Plato and Aristotle* (Baton Rouge: Louisiana State University Press, 1957).

[9] These remarks echo Voegelin without adopting his full analysis.

is that pluralism is not correctly understood as a consequence of relativist and secularist principles but as a mode of experiencing transcendence. Pluralism is the tribute that finitude owes to the Infinite.

A sacral society, whether traditional or reactive, is monolithic and exclusive. Unlike a secular society, it looks to a transcendent source of order as the basis of human society. In other words, it does not find the meaningfulness of human society within human beings themselves, within the range of their own power and achievement. It is monolithic because it acknowledges and allows only one solution to the problem of order on the level of symbol, doctrine, practice, institution and history. The order of society and the meaningfulness of human existence are not open to rational debate leading to reciprocal agreement between clashing viewpoints. To say that the social order has a transcendent source is interpreted to mean that it is given from above and not made by human beings or subject to their alteration or questioning. The absoluteness of the Transcendent is thus transferred by a sacral society to its bodily, historical and institutional expression in a particular social order. Such a society is also exclusive in so far as it cannot in principle without contradicting its own claims allow the legitimacy of other societies. Sacral societies live in an uneasy relationship with one another, if indeed they can be said truly to relate to one another at all. They either coexist in a state of mutual ignorance or isolation or have recourse to war and violence compelling conversion or submission.

At this point, however, I find it useful to make a distinction – suggested by a distinction made by Paul Tillich in another context – between traditional and reactive sacral societies. In dealing with biblical interpretation, Tillich pointed out the difference between the simple literalism that precedes the breaking of the myth and the reactive literalism that follows the widespread recognition that the myth is a myth, not to be taken literally.[10] What from our standpoint we call a simple or naive

---

[10] Paul Tillich, *Dynamics of Faith* (New York: Harper, 1958), pp. 52–4.

literalism is the expression of an undifferentiated consciousness, which has not yet made a distinction between a critically grounded factual statement and other forms of meaning, such as the symbolic, the metaphorical, the fictional. All the different elements are merged in one content of meaning. Strictly speaking, it is not a literalism but an example of compact meaning. That virginal compactness is very different from the aggressive insistence in interpreting the biblical texts as literally factual in a gesture of defence against the critical attempt to differentiate the various forms of meaning and kinds of truth in the Bible. That is indeed literally a literalism, but it represents a sterile, reactive mentality rather than a fruitful pursuit of truth.

I should like to adapt Tillich's distinction, so that it can help us grasp the difference between sacral societies preceding the impact of modernity and sacral societies organized in reaction against that impact. What I have called traditional sacral societies are monolithic and exclusive, because no differentiation has yet been made between the absoluteness of the general source of order and the cultural relativity of a particular order in the concrete. Hence, difference is perceived as evil or defective – to be kept at arm's length lest it corrupt or to be violently resisted if it threatens the existing order. However, it is not easy to maintain such a monolithic and exclusive society in a world of easy communication and universal technology. For that reason the determination to re-establish or purify a sacral society where modernity has already made inroads produces a fiercely intolerant social order, lacking even the modicum of flexibility and openness traditional societies always retained, despite their monolithic structure and exclusiveness. The prime recent example is Khomeini's Iran. Israel manifests some trends in the direction of a reactive, sacral society. However, it is not yet monolithic, and those who want to make it a *halakhic* society do not at present have the power to do so. Nor did the Zionists have in mind the foundation of a religious state. All the same, in its relationship with the Palestinians, Israel does not show itself ready to share political power in a genuinely pluralist society. Whether Jewishness is interpreted religiously or not, when it becomes the exclusive basis for a social order, the society that results, whether secular or pluralist, is a sacral, not a modern society.

We turn now to the other two types of society: the secular and the pluralist. It is not customary to distinguish them. The usual contrast is simply between traditional and modern societies. Further, pluralism is understood to imply secularization, if not a sceptical relativism – not a very helpful attitude with which to approach the problems of the Middle East. 'Give up your religion and become Western secularists' is a prescription that will not be readily accepted.

Modernity is, as we have seen in the first chapter, an ambiguous development, both an advance and a decline, both a growth and a corruption. But what precisely is modernity? A variety of answers has been given, though they do show some convergence and overlapping.

Without denying the correctness of any of the interpretations of modernity, I should like to take as the defining characteristic of modern society that it is understood as the product of free and conscious human agency. Society in the modern conception is the result of free human action. It is not imposed from above as a preformed structure or unalterable sacred order, nor is it determined from below by a necessity of nature. Modern society is regarded as a project to be undertaken by human beings acting freely together in a rational association.

However, the conviction that society is the product, albeit a very imperfect product, of human freedom and rationality may be derived from secularist or religious principles. For a secularist, the source of order in human existence is exclusively immanent. No appeal to a transcendent source is required or legitimate. Human beings are capable of solving the problems of human existence and achieving their own destiny. In any event, lack of capability is not remedied from above. There is no supernatural salvation. Religious eschatology and apocalyptic are interpreted immanently as referring to human history, not to divine intervention. In that conception, secular society is the type of society that excludes religion from the public social order and allows it a function merely in the private sphere.

Strangely enough, the origins of secular society are to be found in Christianity. The initial Christian experience of the Transcendent would seem to have been so overwhelming that it led to an uncompromising dedivinization, falling over into an opposition, between God and the world. In particular, it created the conviction that the religious faith and spiritual destiny of human beings could no longer be represented on earth by political society. Instead, it could be represented only by the Church. This resulted in a whole series of dualisms: Church and Empire, Church and world, religion and politics, the eternal and the temporal, soul and body, man and woman, and so on. In this dualistic thinking, one member was given meaning and value, and the other devalued. Thus Augustine saw temporal affairs as trivial and meaningless, the vicissitudes of political power as of no significance.

What has been happening since the break-up of the medieval order is repeated attempts, often clumsy or ill-directed, to reassert the meaning and value of the world, the temporal, the bodily, the feminine. We can even say, provided we understand it correctly, that the process has been the redivinization of the temporal, not in the sense of identifying God and the world, not in the sense of absolutizing the finite, but in the sense of acknowledging that transcendence always implies immanence and that religious faith should pervade the entirety of human agency and culture. Liberation Theology, for example, is not aiming at a secular society in which religious faith and beliefs are excluded from the public debate and refused a function in the political realm. Politics may be more than the repetitious conflicts of greedy men and women, more than the endless, impotent kicking of unredeemed humanity. Political action may also be the concretization of a graced human agency.

The insight that society is not an unchanging order given, like nature, prior to human freedom, but is the product of human agency has been interpreted in a secularist fashion because of the hardening of Christian faith into a dogmatism and the Christian Church into an authority-structure that excluded dissent. The initial dualism became embodied in a religious institution that arrogated to itself against all other social and political institutions the absoluteness that belongs to religious faith only in its transcendent core, not in its articulation into beliefs and norms. Hence, the assertion that society was a human project, the product of human agency, had to take the form of a separation of Church and State and the exclusion of religion from the public debate.

The medieval order, while seemingly based upon a distinction of Church and State, in fact reconstituted the monolithic character and exclusiveness of a sacral society because of the absolute and total claim of the Christian Church. It provoked a secularist society as its counterpart. However, secularization understood in a limited sense as the dismantling both of church property and of the totalizing and absolutizing structure of traditional beliefs and norms has opened the way for a pluralist society. This third type of society is a project rather than an achievement, but it does represent the emergence of a genuinely political society.

A pluralist society rests upon a process of communication. It aims at consensus, and it sustains and defends itself by argument. A monolithic society rests upon some external authority. It aims at obedience and sustains and defends itself by violence. When religion is integrated into a monolithic society, it legitimates the existing social order and offers religious sanctions against attempts to change it. In a pluralist society, religion has a twofold function. As faith, it keeps the argument open by refusing to absolutize any finite order. As a set of particular beliefs and norms, it offers a rich contribution to the public debate – a contribution that is subject to correction and development but is unsurpassed, none the less, in its scope and depth. In a pluralist society the voice of religion is heard, but so are other voices, which are not silenced or shouted down.

Underlying the turn of religious people to the ideal of a pluralist society are three key insights. First, the recognition, both historically and empirically, that the order of human existence is, in the concrete, the order of a plurality of societies and social groups and that to refuse that plurality in principle, whether within or without a particular society, is to make violence the only recourse where there is a clash of values.

Second, the recognition that the experience of the Transcendent in faith is fundamentally negative in the sense that it brings us no proper content of meaning but has to be expressed in metaphor and symbol; hence, the principle of the equivalence of symbols obtains, which means the truth and efficacy of one symbolic system does not exclude the truth and efficacy of other, different systems. Third, the recognition that the exclusion of political action from the religious sphere because all political action is seen as the essentially meaningless, temporal activity of sinful human beings is a mistaken dualism. Political action is a pre-eminent mode of human agency. It should be redivinized, though not absolutized, as religious *praxis*. Politics can be as much a religious activity as contemplative prayer.

It should be clear, then, that religious language has its place in politics and should not be excluded. Nevertheless, the unqualified assertion of a political claim against others on the basis of religious beliefs that the others do not share is a violation of the nature both of politics and of religious language. Politics seek consensus, and a non-idolatrous religious faith acknowledges the plurality and equivalence of symbols.

Let me end with an example less emotion-laden than the Israeli claim with which I began. I take it from Raimundo Panikkar's foreword to Scott Thomas Eastham's *Nucleus*. He gave it as a typical instance, not as a particular historical case: 'How can American Indians, for instance, present a case against the construction of a highway or atomic power plant on the grounds that their ancestors were buried on the site and that the proposed development would render communication and even personal identification with them impossible?'[11] What does one do with such a claim? It is a political claim made on religious grounds. All the same, people who would summarily dismiss the Israeli claim would be sympathetic to the Amerindian one, even though they did not share the religious beliefs. A reason for the sympathy is that the Amerindians are perceived as being powerless victims of injustice without themselves inflicting injustice upon others, which is not the case with

---

[11]   Scott Thomas Eastham, *Nucleus: Reconnecting Science and Religion in the Nuclear Age*, Foreword by Raimundo Panikkar (Santa Fe, NM: Bear, 1987), p. xxxv.

Israel. All the same, one is still confronted with a politico-economic claim formulated as a religious imperative.

The first thing one must do in a pluralist society is to respect such a claim, not dismiss it or override it as absurd, however little one might share the religious beliefs it presupposes. If that is done, then in many instances some mutual accommodation can be achieved. At the same time, no political claim even religiously formulated, is absolute. The political of its nature is the negotiable, because politics actualizes the human ability not just to act but to act in concert, seeking reciprocal agreement, and this may demand concessions even in one's cherished beliefs. However, there we may anticipate a long process of growth and communication, so that opposing views are taken up into a higher synthesis. Moreover, if politico-religious claims are not absolute, neither are secular claims. For example, the imperative of economic growth through technological development is not an absolute that can override all other claims. In brief, to withdraw any claim, religious or other, from the public debate that constitutes civilized politics is to erect a society upon violence. That may have been an option in the past, but it is a path to suicide for humanity today.

PART III

From the modern subject to the post-modern self

CHAPTER 8

Our new religious identity

It sounds unbelievably banal to say it: but religious people are
going through a crisis of identity today. Catholics, for example,
used to have a clear-cut identity; it is not so now. The reader
will forgive me for referring to myself, but my own case as a
Catholic who publicly broke with his Church is particularly
illustrative. If someone now asks me whether I am a Catholic, I
do not know how to answer. I know that I do not fulfil the
requirements for membership laid down in canon law, nor do I
give assent to all the Catholic dogmas. On the other hand, I
meet acknowledged Catholics who do not take seriously the
canonical conditions for membership and who sometimes
believe fewer Catholic dogmas than I do. Moreover, I am
openly made welcome as a communicating fellow Catholic by
Catholic groups and individuals, clerical and lay, both in
North America and Britain. That could not have happened a
few decades ago. What criteria should I use to decide my
possible Catholic identity?

Again, whom should one recognize as a Christian today? A
book appears, such as *The Myth of God Incarnate*,[1] edited by the
Christian theologian John Hick, denying a central Christian
doctrine: the Incarnation in the sense in which it was defined
by the Church Councils. There is a traditional response from
some Christians, denouncing the authors as having apostatized
from the Christian faith, but as the wider response shows there
is not among the general body of those who call themselves
Christians any consensus now at the doctrinal level. How, then,

[1] London: SCM Press, 1977.

131

do we determine a Christian identity? In some ways, I might add, it is easier to decide whether a person belongs to a particular Christian denomination than whether he is a Christian. The criteria for belonging to a denomination are usually external and easily applied, but not all who attend the services and pay their contributions would regard themselves as believers in Christ.

The problem is not just the seeming erosion of Christian identity in a secular culture. It is also the widening or, should one say, the blurring of the religious identity of Christians by the acceptance of other religions. Raimundo Panikkar declares that he is not only fully a Christian but also fully a Hindu. One could also argue whether the last teaching of Thomas Merton was Christian or Buddhist and perhaps conclude that he himself would not at the end have wanted to have made that distinction. If, however, Christians no longer regard the Christian tradition as the sole or final depository of religious truth and value, does not their identity as religious persons lie at a deeper level than their distinctively Christian mentality and behaviour, deeper than their profession of Christian faith?

So far religious identity has been the theme, but a parallel set of problems is present today in the social and political field. Allow me again to refer to myself. Where do I place my ultimate political allegiance? I am from England, but that is not now my home. Does Canada, the country of my citizenship, claim my final loyalty? But Canada rests upon a constitutional arrangement and has not the unity of a people or *Volk*. As a political construct, it may possibly come to an end. If so, I shall have to appeal to a deeper level to forge a new political identity for myself. To take other examples – many black Americans are now feeling a greater identity with black Africans than with their fellow white Americans. In a different vein, the executive of a multi-national corporation no longer has a social identity circumscribed by a particular nation. Likewise, those working in one of the agencies of the United Nations, with men and women of many nations, all committed to social and political interests that are transnational, presumably begin to feel the pressure of loyalties that transcend patriotism. The same may be said of people working for the World Council of Churches; it affects both their political and their religious identity.

To call oneself a citizen of the world is unreal, because there is as yet no world order. But the movement towards one already relativizes particular national, regional and cultural identities. There is indeed a growing stress upon those particular identities, but that is because they are threatened. We are subjected to the pressure of a pluralistic social world before we have fully internalized the reality of the particular social group into which we are born. The tradition which should mould our particular identity is relativized and thus rendered largely ineffective before it can do its work. In earlier times one grew up into a limited social world from which one might, when fully formed, enter into relation with other cultures. Young people today come under the sway of exotic cultural elements and even create an international youth culture without having assimilated the culture of their birth. Religiously, many are learning about other religions and adopting their practices before they have known, let alone practised, their own.

There is today, it seems, an unresolved tension between a growing and desirable universalism and the need for a particular social identity and tradition. The universalism checks a destructive political particularism and, rejecting cultural and religious exclusivism, prevents people from being enclosed within the boundaries of a limited social or religious world. The contemporaneous clinging to particularity expresses the need for roots. It is also a reaction against a corrosive pluralism, which by bombarding people with a multiplicity of cultural elements prevents them from grasping the full reality and quality of any. Drawn by a universalism, seemingly demanded by the next phase of human political and cultural development, yet unwilling to relinquish a particularity, serving to protect the rich variety of human life against homogenization into a thinly textured world culture, represented by a Hilton in every city, people find themselves with a confused identity. Universalism is destroying the particularity needed to nourish it; particularity, especially in the political order, is threatening the universalism needed for human survival, not just for progress. Can the two be reconciled?

Where lies the basic identity of a person or social entity? At the universal or particular level? Put it in the concrete with reference to religion: am I through and through a Christian, who then as a Christian enters into a relationship with people of other religions? Or does my religious faith at its depths have a universal quality that unites me there with all men of faith, even though my faith finds a particular social and historical embodiment in Christian forms and institutions? Am I religious because I am a Christian or Christian because I am religious? And if both are true, how does the dialectic between them work itself out?

The problem of religious identity is acute today because that identity is breaking through to a new consciousness and new forms. This chapter will first examine the general question of personal and collective identity, and then apply its findings. In doing this, it will be making use of some ideas from Habermas and through him from Kohlberg. I acknowledge here my debt to them. However, let me add that my purpose is not the exposition of their thought, but the application of it to answer my own questions.[2]

To begin with personal identity – personal identity may be defined as the capability of conscious subjects to remain identical with themselves, despite changes that affect the structure of their personality. It is the unity and continuity of self-consciousness. Persons as conscious subjects are repeatedly faced with situations that challenge the existing structure of their consciousness – in other words, which contradict the way they feel, the way they think, the way they act. They can meet those situations and cope with the experiences they involve only by reconstructing their personality or acquiring a new self,

[2]   The most accessible text is probably Jürgen Habermas, 'Moral development and ego identity', in Jürgen Habermas, *Communication and the Evolution of Society* (Boston: Beacon Press, 1979), pp. 69–96. See also, Charles Davis 'Pluralism, privacy and the interior self', *Theology and Political Society* (Cambridge: Cambridge University Press, 1980), Chapter 7. This chapter has also been published in Don S. Browning and Francis Schüssler-Fiorenza, eds., *Habermas, Modernity and Public Theology* (New York: Crossroad, 1992).

as we say. Personal identity is the basic unity, underlying the series of particular identities imposed on us by the conflicts, contradictions and challenges of living through change. Where there is personal identity, all those particular identities can be brought within the continuity of a single life-history, within the unity of a single self-consciousness.

Personal identity, as also collective identity, is a normative concept, not just descriptive. It is not used merely to describe a state of affairs, but to express an ideal to be striven for, a value to be embodied. For that reason, we can speak of a 'loss of identity', an 'identity crisis', of a 'weak identity', and so on. In the same fashion, we can measure the extent to which a person has reached an identity appropriate to a human being by marking off stages in the unfolding of personal identity. Three such stages may be distinguished: pre-conventional or natural identity, conventional identity or an identity of roles, and post-conventional or universalistic identity. This is, of course, an abstract scheme. Development in the concrete will show unevenness and internal inconsistencies.

At the pre-conventional level, the child learns to distinguish its body as a bounded, durable organism from the environment. Through its body as delimited in space, persisting through time and existing over against surrounding objects, the child apprehends itself as a distinct self. However, at this stage, the child does not make any difference between physical objects and social objects. It has not yet entered into the social world with its meanings. The human meanings that constitute social relationships and social institutions escape it. Other persons and itself as a distinct organism are just objects like the other natural objects in the environment. Its identity may therefore be called a natural identity.

At the next stage, the conventional level, the person learns those clusters of social meanings we call roles. A role constitutes a symbolic identity. It attaches to the person a stable set of expectations concerning behaviour. These expectations may be formulated as norms or concrete rules of conduct. They are conventions to which the person must conform in order to carry out the role or roles society assigns. When the person follows the conventions and thus fulfils the expectations of society, he or she receives an acknowledgement of his or her social role. That acknowledgement is internalized as a conventional identity. It is bound up with a reciprocal acknowledgement by the person of the social roles of others. A conventional identity or identity of roles is the entry into the network of social relationships.

Corresponding to the conventional stage in the development of personal identity is the conventional type of moral consciousness. Moral consciousness at the conventional level is focused upon the observance of norms, that is, of concrete moral rules. It is a morality of conformity, with an orientation towards external authority. Two sub-stages may be distinguished. The person first emerges with a conventional identity in the family and in the other small social groups, such as the peer group. In that context what directs and reinforces the person in casting his or her conduct in stereotype roles is the approval and disapproval of those personally met and interacted with. In the second sub-stage the person moves into the wider society. Conventional morality becomes conformity to the law and order of the social system, an internalization of its norms or rules of conduct and submission to the authority of its institutions.

The person breaks through from a conventional identity to a post-conventional or universalistic identity by an advance in reflection, bringing a distinction between norms or concrete rules on the one hand and the universal principles that generate the norms or rules on the other.

A universalistic identity is not tied to any particular role or set of roles; it goes behind all of them to the principles that create them. With a merely conventional identity the loss of a role is a loss of personal identity, and the person is thrown into a state of crisis. That is not so with a universalistic identity, which consists in the capability of creating ever new identities in coping with personal shifts within the role-system of society and, at a deeper level, with the conflicts and contradictions that result in changes in the role-system itself. The basic identity of the person is no longer indissolubly bound up with any particular set of norms, rules, institutions or traditions. It is an identity that can survive the most radical changes history may inflict upon the person. That is not to say that the person ever exists apart from a particular identity with its norms and conventional elements, nor will any change, however great, ever bring a total break between tradition or the past conventions and the present or new conventions. All the same, a person with a universalistic identity has by reflection penetrated to the springs of human creativity, from which human beings draw in constructing their successive social worlds, with their roles, norms, institutions and traditions. The person grounds his or her identity at that level and is thus capable of making the transition from one social role or order to another social role or order.

A post-conventional or universalistic identity is accompanied by a post-conventional or universalistic moral consciousness. This no longer focuses upon norms or concrete moral rules, but upon the principles lying behind the rules. For that reason, the orientation is not to external authority, which is now replaced by a personal autonomy.

The universalistic moral consciousness is found in different degrees of realization. The lowest degree, while universalistic in the sense of moving behind conventional norms to general principles, is at the same time individualistic in orientation. Each person follows his or her own interests under the utilitarian assumption that the pursuit of private interests by each member results in the general good of society. An egocentric freedom for the individual is held to be compatible with such egocentric freedom for all. Society is viewed in terms of a social contract among independent persons. The practical medium for the reconciliation of individual interests is the law with its regulation and sanctioning of contracts, and the universal principles lying behind particular norms and rules are conceived legalistically. This first degree of universalistic morality corresponds to the outlook of bourgeois liberalism, described by C. B. MacPherson as a possessive individualism. Each person regards himself or herself as an independent owner of his or her person and talents. Society is a system of contractual exchange among autonomous proprietors. It is a market view of society.

Two remarks may be made about that outlook. First, historically the economic realm was the first area of society to free itself from the restrictive bonds of traditional convention and to become organized on universal principles. Bourgeois liberalism was the beginning of the breakup of political particularism. But, second, it represents the kind of universalism people rightly fear, because it produces rootless, competitive, egoistic individuals, having no organic relationship to any social group. It was a one-sided development that indeed freed human economic activity from the restraints imposed by the rigidity of unchanging conventions and institutions, but the universalistic creative force it released was competitive and individualistic. That force has worked and is still working up to the destruction of the deeper universality that unites human beings, instead of isolating them from one another.

But there are higher forms of universalism.

The next degree of universalistic moral consciousness is when the person advances to a grasp of universal ethical principles. The person no longer acts on the basis of private interest; it is not enough that the private interests of all individuals should be co-ordinated legally. What guides conduct is personal conscience as the consciousness of universal moral values, formulated as universally valid moral principles. Conscience at this stage is autonomous. The person does not consider it moral simply to conform to the accepted standards of behaviour. It is not an adequate justification of conduct to point to existing conventions. The conventions or accepted norms must themselves be tested against conscience, that is, against universal principles. The norms or concrete rules institutionalized in a society and governing its culture may be understood as a particular interpretation of human needs and interest. They are moral norms, obligating men and women in their conscience, only in so far as they truly embody universal human needs and interests and are not the open or disguised expression of the exclusive interests of an individual or social group. The person with an autonomous conscience critically examines the currently accepted norms of behaviour to assess whether they can be subsumed under general ethical principles, the aim of which is to abstract and formulate the universalizable features of human needs and interests. The autonomy of the person is an autonomy of conscience, and this stage may thus be seen as the stage of personal moral freedom.

It might be thought that moral development ended there, and that indeed corresponds to the point at which Kohlberg completes his account of the stages of moral consciousness. But Habermas with some reason thinks it necessary to add a further degree of development at the post-conventional level. What has been said so far leaves the individual person to test norms against universal principles by himself or herself – in a monologue, as it were, within the individual conscience. That would not seem to correspond either to the social character of human nature or to the criterion of universality as applied to norms. Can, for instance, the individuals of one social group take adequate account of the needs and interests of those in other social groups? It is possible to grant that an individual may avoid canonizing selfish interests as moral values. It is much more difficult to suppose that he or she alone can transcend the basis of his or her social group, so that the interpretation of needs and interests and the resulting scale of moral values reach a truly universal level and do not impose upon humanity as a whole the conventional morality of a particular society or class. We are now critical of the class bias of some moralities making universal claims, and women have recently been pointing out the sexist bias of current moral teaching. The autonomy of the individual conscience is too weak of itself to bring about a fully universalistic moral consciousness.

What is wanted is a social procedure, open in principle to all, for the testing of normative claims. The normative claims to be tested include norms both in the sense of concrete rules and allegedly universal moral principles. The social procedure for their examination should be appropriate to morally free persons at a post-conventional level of development, ready to reach an agreement, but refusing any demand simply to conform. We are therefore speaking of a process of communication among autonomous persons, who as such participate equally and freely in a communication unconstrainted by domination. Communication or social dealings among people take place on two levels. At the level of action normative claims are by and large taken for granted. If, however, they are called into question and become problematical, a second level of communication, namely discourse, is required to argue out differences and re-establish agreement. If discourse is to justify moral norms and principles in a manner that takes up into itself but transcends the working of the individual autonomous conscience, it must be universal and allow a free and equal participation. The universality, equality and freedom represent an ideal to be striven for, not a factual accomplishment, but the need constantly to strive for that ideal acts as a moral criterion. A concrete moral issue, for instance, is undoubtedly not settled until all those whose interests are involved have freely had their say.

Only a society of freedom, justice and equality could give the testing of its norms and values over to free and open discourse among all. It would be a truly emancipated society that succeeded in institutionalizing unconstrained communication about moral values as the basis of its social order. As the culmination of human moral development, we are asking for a social and political order in which human beings as free persons are bound together in a communicative network of interaction and discourse, unimpeded and undistorted by oppression. Then norms and principles can receive their only appropriate grounding in the free consensus of autonomous persons inter-acting without external constraint. The previous degree of a universalistic moral consciousness was called that of personal moral freedom. This, the final one, may be entitled that of moral and political freedom. Through striving to approximate to that ideal, the post-conventional or universalistic identity of the human person reaches its greatest realization.

A distinction has been made between norms or concrete moral rules and the moral principles on which they depend. A further distinction is now relevant between the basic principles – roughly speaking, freedom, justice and equality – implicit in the structure of human communication itself and the general body of moral principles as reached in the communicative process. Moral development may then be understood as an increase in self-reflection in regard to human action. The transition from the natural to the conventional level occurs when, in reflection, a distinction is made between human actions and the norms or rules that govern their meaning. The person passes from the conventional to the post-conventional level through distinguishing norms or concrete moral rules and the universal moral principles lying behind them. The final degree of moral self-reflection comes with the distinction between the principles implied in the very process of human communication and the principles established by that process.

A consideration of the development of personal identity has already raised questions concerning society. How, in fact, can a universalistic structure of personal identity arise and be sustained unless the basic institutions of a society embody universal principles? But before turning directly to the matter of collective identity, I want to say something about the application of what has been said about personal identity and moral consciousness to the present religious situation.

The key distinction is obviously that between a conventional and a post-conventional identity.

Traditional religious people have a conventional identity. Their religious identity is tied to the fixed contents of a tradition, to its institutions and practices. They subordinate themselves to the authority of the documents and representatives of their tradition.Their fundamental attitude is one of conformity to the formulated teaching, established practices and consecrated officials of their religious community. This conformism is reinforced rather than weakened by the insistence that external compliance is not enough, but that internal obedience is required for a genuine faith. Any substantial change in the normative content and rules of the tradition is experienced as a loss of identity and, consequently, is fiercely resisted. History shows that such a conventional religious identity may flourish in a naive fashion while simply ignoring the existence of other traditions and thus evading the reflection which a taking cognizance of their existence would provoke.

Where, however, it is maintained in the teeth of other traditions, it results in an exclusiveness that attaches the absoluteness of religious faith to the particularities of a single tradition.

The present situation is that for many it has become increasingly difficult to maintain a religious stance of a conventional
kind. The reason is not simply the internal development of
religious consciousness; though such development has its part,
provoked by the tension between the universal and absolute
features of religious faith and the particularity and relativity of
every tradition. Nor is it enough to add the impact of historical
criticism and what Peter Berger, I think, called the 'debunking'
effect of the social sciences. People are affected who in their
religious life usually disregard the views of theologians and
academics on religion, counting any departure from orthodoxy
as a professional liability. The factor with the widest influence
here in upsetting conventional religion is the pressure of
universalistic trends in other areas of culture, so that a conventional religious identity has become an anomaly, incompatible
not so much with the content as with the structure of modern
consciousness.

The capitalist economic system continues to ride roughshod
over political and cultural particularities, creating its own
limited type of universal order. Science and technology make
transcultural claims and have in fact gained a universally
acknowledged validity. The rapid pace of social change resulting from scientific technology forces people to make a reflective
distinction between the universal and the particular, between
universal principles and particular instances of their realization. They become used to seeing every object as a replaceable
and improvable instance of a general technical solution or
procedure. The increase in world communications made possible by technology plunges people into a plurality of cultures.
They cope with the experience by relativizing particular
cultural manifestations and more or less spontaneously seeking
the universal underlying the particular. In brief, people today
are, willy-nilly, thrust into a post-conventional outlook. It has
already been indicated that the universalism that results is not

an unmixed blessing, but its defects have to be met by further development, not by regression.

What happens to religion of a conventional kind in a universalistic context? It can cause a split identity, which segregates religion and some sections of morality from other areas of human experience. Religion indeed can become a security blanket in the midst of a bewildering universalism. But the segregation of religious faith inflicts a loss of reality upon its objects. Where the reality-loss is not compensated for by fanaticism, religion becomes traditional practice without genuine belief.

The move to a universalistic identity may mean a complete dissolution of religious faith and practice. There are some thinkers for whom religion is essentially a conventional mode of consciousness, so that the shift to a universalistic morality and the rationalization of social life means the end of religion. Those who resist that conclusion have to show that religious faith is capable of bearing the increase of reflection that distinguishes between universal religious principles and the particular religious tradition. The universal principles are the creative source of the symbols and stories, the institutions and teachings, the rites and norms of each tradition, but are not limited to any single tradition nor exhausted by the already completed history of them all. The genuinely new is still possible. Those who have reached a post-conventional religious identity by grounding themselves upon universal religious principles are capable of positively accepting the plurality of religious traditions and substantial changes in their own tradition. Their basic religious identity is not threatened, because it is not tied to the formulated content of the tradition to which they belong.

But they will belong to a tradition – unless their universalism is of a crude and inadequate kind. The religious counterpart of bourgeois liberalism, though some professedly radical students do not realize it, is the attempt to construct one's own individual religion with elements from a diversity of cultures. A mature universalism is a degree of self-reflection sufficient to allow one to discern the distinction between the universal and the particular in the tradition which is one's own. It does not mean distancing oneself from any organic relation to any tradition. Not to belong to any tradition is to fall into an abstract and empty universalism – abstract, because it is limited to formal and thus repeatable features of culture; empty, because it lacks the unique concrete substance of cultural reality. The eclecticism of do-it-yourself religion is an attempt to fill that emptiness.

Granted that a universalistic religious identity is compatible with belonging to a tradition, such an identity does however mean that one's attitude to the tradition is not an attitude of conformity but an attitude of critical appropriation. The person's religious faith reflects an autonomy of conscience, so that the contents and norms of the tradition are subject to a critical examination and open to modification and rejection. When a universalistic identity has become reflectively explicit, there is no longer need of the mental gymnastics frequently found in religious traditions as they endeavour to show that the tradition has always been right and has not in any respect substantially changed.

Here, however, we confront the same difficulty as with moral consciousness. The autonomy of the individual conscience is insufficient as the principle of a fully universalistic outlook. If each individual is left to make a personal adaptation of the particular religious tradition, then the result will show the blindness and prejudice of the individual's social group. The individual cannot simply by a monologue within his or her own personal consciousness move beyond the cultural limitations of the social group to the realm of the truly universal. The individual must communicate with others in an ongoing process of communication – a communication in principle unrestricted or open to all and unconstrained by domination, that is, the equality of participation is unchecked by the invocation of privilege or the exercise of authority. A post-conventional or universalistic religious identity is therefore realized when people, belonging to a religious tradition but not tied to its fixed contents or norms, engage as free, autonomous persons in a process of unrestricted and unconstrained communication with others of the same tradition, of other traditions, or of no tradition on matters concerning religion with the aim of achieving agreement, not conformity. But to complete the analysis, we must turn from the question of personal identity to that of collective identity.

The stages in the development of human society do not exactly correspond to the stages of personal development. Individuals may reach a higher stage of development than that common to most members of their society and may therefore be out of harmony with contemporary social institutions and life. On the other hand, the individual may fail to reach the level of development needed to participate effectively and creatively in the life of society. But, more than that, an unevenness of development is a more marked and more influential feature of social history than of personal history. One set of institutions in a society may be operating at one level of development, while another set is operating at a higher or lower level. The classification of societies is therefore a matter requiring a complex assessment. However, having said all that and having apologized for the oversimplification, I am, following Habermas, going to distinguish four stages of social evolution in the matter of collective identity. Collective identity concerns the manner in which a society secures its unity and continuity through change. It affects personal identity, which the person achieves through socialization, though, as we have seen, the dynamics of personal development works to give the person an independence over against the social system. Personal identity is a social identity, in so far as a person identifies with a particular social reality.

The first stage of social evolution was that of archaic societies, which had a structure based on kinship ties. The kinship ties were elaborated into mythical world views, which established similarities among all objects, not distinguishing physical and social objects nor persons, animals and things. Everything was brought into an order by an extended kinship system. Since the tribe was not distinguished from nature, nor the individual from the tribe, society at this stage may be said to have had a natural identity. There was no awareness as yet of the distinction between concrete actions on the one hand, and social roles and moral norms on the other. Nor were symbols distinguished from natural objects. Both moral and religious consciousness remained, therefore, at the pre-conventional level, where the world of nature and the world of human meaning are not differentiated.

The second stage was that of the early civilizations. It was marked by the rise of a centralized political organization, either as kingdom or as city-state, and the emergence of a class structure of society. At this stage, social roles, with the norms governing them, were consciously differentiated from concrete actions, so that a conventional identity or identity of roles became generally possible. The social order, being now a power-structure, required legitimation. This was given it by including a justificatory account of it in the religious narratives and by consecrating it through ritual. No distinction was made between the religious and the political community, with the consequence that religious identity coincided with political identity. It was a conventional identity, based upon conformity to the established or traditional social order and demanding the obedient performance of the roles assigned within it.

A breakthrough from conventional identity came in the period of the high civilizations or great empires with the rise of the universal religions. The universal religions, particularly monotheism, mark a new stage of social evolution, because they led to the formation of a personal identity severed from all concrete roles and norms. The religious community no longer coincided with the political community, but was a potentially universal community, embracing people under different political regimes. Personal identity was thus released from exclusive determination by the roles and norms of a particular society. In monotheism the person was conceived of as having his or her own identity as standing before God and therefore as constituted fully as an individual in relation to God. Thus, in the development of religious meaning there emerged the conception of the singular person in a universal community, and an identity of roles was transcended by a universalistic identity.

But this achievement, available on the personal level, was in contradiction with the political systems of the time, which remained particularistic. The conflict had to be covered over by ideology.

The tension between a universalistic personal identity, introduced and fostered by systems of religious meaning, and political particularism has persisted down to the present. The problem, however, was kept latent until the modern era by several factors, which have now lost their force. There was the persistence of elements of an earlier type, which in their exclusive particularity blunted religious universalism. However, the working of the universalistic principles of religion has gradually eliminated those earlier elements. Again, a distinction was made between actual members of the religious community and those outside as still to be converted. The outsiders, though potentially members, could for the time being be treated in good conscience as political enemies. But the breakup of the one Christian Church into different Churches, the coming of religious toleration and the consequent voluntary character of religious association, all have reduced the social and institutional side of Church membership; it has become more a private affair, which cannot be put to political use. Lastly, a dualistic outlook was content with a spiritual universalism, confined to the Church, while the secular world with the State was given over to political conflicts and divisions. For several decades now that dualism has been strongly resisted by Christians, with insistence upon the social and political implications of the Christian faith. In the modern era, then, religious universalism and the continuing political particularism stand in open contradiction.

Nowadays, however, a universalistic personal identity is no longer necessarily or even generally religious in character. In our secular culture religious faith for many has been taken up without remainder into a universalistic morality, with no religious doctrines or ritual. There is also the inadequate but very influential type of universalism promoted by economic liberalism. In other words, whatever its historical origins, a universalistic personal identity is a common achievement in modern secular culture, not a distinctive attribute of a religious consciousness.

The fourth stage of social evolution, the modern age, is characterized by the cleavage between personal identity, universal in its structure and norms, and the collective identity, still particularistic in structure and rules of behaviour, of the various social and political communities. How can human beings move to a new type of collective identity, which would no longer exclude people as outsiders, but would relate to them as other?

Socially and politically, the way forward, as Habermas sees it, lies in the recognition that human society today cannot achieve a rational identity within the boundaries of any permanent collective body, with its particular territory or organization. Our basic social identity cannot come from membership in a stable collective entity, confronting us as fixed objective reality. Such a social identity is incompatible with our universalistic personal identity. Instead of consisting in membership of a fixed collective body, collective identity at its basic level lies in a process of universal communication, uniting human beings without distinction in the shaping of a new collective will, in the creation of new collective identities at the level of concrete action, in the formation of a new global order. For our basic social and political identity today we must go beyond all our established social and political units and relate ourselves to a deeper social reality, the creative source of all particular social institutions when these can lay claim to rationality: communicative interaction and discourse among free persons. Since membership in a state, nation or race does not give people their basic social identity, they will not regard non-members primarily as outsiders, but will relate to them as simply others, who have to participate equally with them in the task of shaping a collective will for humanity through universal communication.

The same approach to collective identity is valid within the religious realm. Membership of a permanent religious body that confronts us as a fixed objective entity cannot give us our basic social identity as religious persons. No church or other religious social entity can constitute the fundamental level of religious collective identity. It is not merely that membership of a particular Christian denomination can no longer be regarded as fundamental, but also that belonging to the divided Christian Church as a social reality distinct from other religious bodies has ceased to constitute the fundamental level. What is being uncovered as the basic level for a religious collective identity is that world-wide process of communication which in other contexts we refer to as the religious history of humankind. It is becoming more and more a matter of explicit awareness that there is a single total history of human religiousness; or, to put it in another way, that the history of particular religious traditions becomes fully intelligible only when seen in the context of a universal religious history. There is an increasing convergence of religious traditions. Making one's own the ongoing, convergent history of religious faith by participating in a process of free, equal and universal communication among people striving without domination to reach agreement on religious concerns is how one achieves a basic social identity of a religious kind at the level of the present situation. That does not mean, as I tried to make clear in dealing with personal identity, that people should cease to belong to particular traditions and their social institutions. There is need of an organic relation to a particular tradition, both for personal growth and for the rich individuality of concrete religious faith. True universality does not abolish, but grounds and sustains plurality. But it does mean a degree of self-reflection that distinguishes between the particularity of the tradition and its universal base and also places that particularity in the wider context of human religious history. It also means that no already formed religious body can claim a self-sufficient collective identity nor maintain that to be a member of it should constitute the basic social identity of a religious person.

The present religious situation requires more than the adaptation of what already exists. It calls for the creation of new forms and new institutions. None of the major problems confronting the human race – such as the formation of a world order to make nuclear disarmanent possible, the ecological crisis, economic injustice and world poverty, race prejudice and the position of women – can be solved within the boundaries and resources of any one tradition. Traditions must converge to produce together new solutions. Only by going behind a conventional identity in both its personal and collective realization to a post-conventional, universalistic identity, personal and collective, as grounded in the structure of human communication, will that be possible.

The problems just instanced are not specifically religious problems. Nevertheless, they exemplify the kind of problems religious people should be concerned with. For purposes of exposition I have spoken separately of religious identity as if it were something apart from personal and social identity. But it is not. Religious identity designates the articulation of a religious dimension implicit in the achievement of personal and social identity.

Human communication as I have understood it here is not the mere passing on of information. It is an intersubjective relationship among free, fully individual persons, sharing their experiences and knowledge in interaction and discourse, with the aim of mutual understanding and agreement. Reflection upon the presuppositions or conditions of possibility of human communication in that sense brings us up against two limit-problems. By a limit-problem is meant a problem that points us beyond the limits of human meaning.

The first is the constitution of the individual person as an absolute or unconditional value. This is presupposed by human communication in the analysis I have cited. Communicative action is distinct from instrumental action, which uses human persons like things as instruments in achieving success in some undertaking. It is also distinct from strategic action, which takes account of the other person's intentions and plans, but simply in order to counter them and adapt them to one's own game plan. In communicative action the person goes out to meet another person in a mutual relationship in which each recognizes the other as an equal, independent self, who cannot be subordinated to any external purpose and who is therefore of unconditional worth. But how can that unconditional worth be grounded? This is a pertinent question today when some are proclaiming the end of the individual, contending that the individual is an obsolete social factor when society can be run much more efficiently on the basis of systems-theory and with the use of the computer. Can the dignity of the individual as an absolute value be retained without a relation to the Absolute? I suggest that the individual is of unconditional worth, because at the deepest level the personal self is one with Absolute Reality.

The second problem that confronts human communication is the death of its participants. Death threatens the very meaning of human communication, because it apparently renders impossible the kind of relationship sought with other selves. In that relationship we are joined to other persons unconditionally in an intersubjective union to which we owe our own identity and growth. What are we to do when our partners in communication are annihilated by death? Erase them from our memory? That would be an evasion of reality. But can we hold them in remembrance if there is no basis in reality for a continuing communion with them? Something as limited as material comfort retains its trivial degree of meaning in face of death. But can the wealth of meaning attached to human community remain intact if human community is conceived as eventually passing into nothingness with the continuous, successive annihilation of all its participants? Here Christians and Jews may recall that their God is a God of the living and the dead and a God who creates human community. They can conceive of God as the saving reality met with in human communication as its ground. Human communication is a more than human achievement when it is understood as between free persons united in a union undistorted by domination. It is in fact the description of salvation to be received as a transcendent gift.

These are but hints and suggestions for the transposition of some traditional religious themes into terms corresponding to a modern problematic. They demand a more careful and more detailed elaboration than is possible here. The chief concern here has been with the preliminary task of showing the way beyond the conventional level of religious faith and identity at which many people, including not a few church leaders, are stuck. A post-conventional, universalistic religious identity, both personal and social, not tied to the fixed contents and norms of any one tradition nor to any permanent collective body, alone corresponds to the present level of human social development. Personal autonomy is not a rebellion, but the gift of the Spirit. Conformity is not a virtue, but a lack of confidence in the Spirit that makes us free. A communication open to all as free persons and undistorted by domination is the descent of the Spirit of love.

CHAPTER 9

Post-modernity and the formation of the self

In a much-noticed Aquinas Lecture, given at Marquette University in 1968, Bernard Lonergan discussed the shift of attention from the metaphysics of the soul to the analysis of the subject.[1] The metaphysics of the soul is a totally objective account of the constituents of human nature, applying universally to all human beings, whatever may be their state of mind or degree of development. The study of the subject concerns oneself insasmuch as one is conscious. Its results, therefore, vary according to the level of consciousness. Furthermore, it is possible to neglect the subject and remain in a state of self-ignorance. On the other hand, self-reflection will uncover the existential subject, namely the subject not merely as a knower, but also as a doer; indeed, more than that, a doer engaged in a self-making. The subject freely and responsibly makes the self to be as a particular self.

What Lonergan is doing in that lecture is inviting us to rethink Thomism in the context of modernity. The modern age was inaugurated by Kant, with his Copernican revolution or turn to the subject, and continued by Fichte, Hegel, Kierkegaard and others who worked within the paradigm of the philosophy of consciousness. From that standpoint, modernity may be identified with the affirmation of an autonomous, self-legislating, self-related subject and the insistence upon a doctrine of immanence that refuses submission to anything that attempts to impose itself heteronomously from without as

[1] The lecture is reprinted in William F. Ryan and Bernard J. Tyrrell, eds., *A Second Collection: Papers by Bernard J. F. Lonergan* (London: Darton, Longman & Todd, 1974), pp. 69–86.

knowledge or value. Lonergan, with the priority he gives to cognitional theory over metaphysics and his finding in consciousness the data for an invariant basis of human knowledge and for an unrevisable cognitional theory, is clearly trying to resituate Thomism within the philosophy of consciousness.

What is ironic is that the attempt comes at a time when modernity is under attack from a variety of angles and when everyone is now talking of post-modernity. It will be helpful, I think, to clarify the use of the terms 'modern' and 'postmodern' before examining that feature of post-modernity that concerns us most here, namely the death or disappearance of the self.

The term 'post-modern' was first used in the late fifties in a literary context to deplore the diminishing influence of the modernist movement. Then in the seventies it became a catchword in architecture, theatre, painting, film and music. Aesthetically it expresses a reaction against the modernist insistence upon formal purity and against the modernist contempt for mass culture. Hence post-modernism is characterized by a disturbing mixture of styles, with ideas, images and motifs plundered from various sources.[2]

Philosophically, the situation is more confused, because of the ambiguity of post-structuralism and the question of the continuity or discontinuity between the modern and the postmodern. Structuralism is itself post-modern in its refusal of the modern focus upon the subject. It is a move from subject to system, from an exploration of conscious intentionality to the permanent, unconscious structures of the mind. At the same time, structuralism shares with modernity the stress upon rationality and upon the rational demand for unity, objectivity and universality. In contrast, Derrida and the deconstructionists are both post-structuralist and post-modern. They are poststructuralist in their rejection of the idea of objectively given, invariant structures. They are post-modern in their refusal of

---

[2] Cf. David Ingram, *Habermas and the Dialectic of Reason* (New Haven and London: Yale University Press, 1987), Chapter 6: 'Discourse on modernity: a philosophical interlude'.

the unity and universality of truth. They replace the quest for final meaning and grounded truth with the endless play of significations as releasing a limitless multiplicity of meanings. The Western philosophical tradition is dismissed as an illusory metaphysics of presence, that is, it is built upon the illusion that reason can leave behind language and reach the pure presence of truth and reality. Derrida dubs Western metaphysics as logocentric and as phonocentric. It is logocentric because it assigns the origin of truth to the *logos*, both the classical *logos* as the voice of reason and the Christian *logos* as the voice of God. The *logos* was pre-eminently the spoken word. Speech was regarded as primary and writing as secondary under the illusion that speech communicates presence. Thus, logocentrism, or the claim to extra-linguistic truth, and phonocentrism, or the exaltation of the spoken word as the immediate presence of reality, imply one another. The rejection of both by Derrida marks a clear break with the Western philosophical tradition as a whole, not merely with the post-Kantian epoch.

Another formulation of post-modernity is given by the French theorist, Jean-François Lyotard.[3] For him post-modernity means incredulity towards all meta-narratives. What characterizes modern science as modern is its self-legitimation in second-order or meta-discourse, and such legitimation, as in Habermas, leads to an appeal to some grand narrative, such as the narrative of the emancipation of the rational subject. Lyotard remains incredulous towards the universalistic claims of the great narratives of modernity. His contrast between scientific knowledge and narrative knowledge would seem at first sight to be positivistic. However, his objection is not to first-order or popular narrative, but to the insistence upon the need for legitimation, with the consequent creation of meta-narratives. There is no such need, Lyotard argues. Popular narratives should be allowed to fulfil their function of holding together our culture with no further appeal to legitimation or meta-narratives. For Habermas, to give up in that way universalistic claims would be to leave the social hopes of liberal

[3] Jean-François Lyotard, *La Condition postmoderne: Rapport sur le savoir* (Paris: Les Editions de Minuit, 1979).

politics without rational grounding and thus abandon the
elements of reason in modernity. We should be left with merely
a context-dependent social criticism. While Habermas would
seem to be clinging to a universalistic philosophy to save liberal
politics, his French critics are prepared to give up liberal
politics in order to avoid a universalistic philosophy.

Habermas, it should be clear, continues to support modernity and is opposed to some of the key post-modern conten-
tions. He has caused some irritation by assigning the post-
moderns to the neo-conservative camp. But his position is more
nuanced than it first appears. He speaks of modernity as 'an
incomplete project'[4] and maintains that a counter-discourse
against some features of modernity has been part of modernity
from its beginning. His is not an unconditional acceptance.
What is the project of modernity? He gives this very clear
statement:

The project of modernity formulated in the 18th century by the
philosophers of the Enlightenment consisted in their efforts to develop
objective science, universal morality and law, and autonomous art
according to their inner logic. At the same time, this project intended
to release the cognitive potentials of each of these domains from their
esoteric forms. The Enlightenment philosophers wanted to utilize this
accumulation of specialized culture for the enrichment of everyday
life – that is to say, for the rational organization of everyday social
life.[5]

But the optimism of the Enlightenment thinkers was not
fulfilled. The project led to the fragmentation of culture and to
a growing distance between the culture of the experts and that
of the larger public, with the increasing impoverishment of the
life-world. The key to the correction and consequent completion of the problem of modernity lies, according to Habermas, in the right understanding of subjectivity.

Habermas considers that the paradigm of the subject-
centred philosophy of consciousness is finished. It is exhausted.
The only way forward is by its replacement by the intersubjec-

---

[4] See the title of his talk, 'Modernity – an incomplete project', reprinted in Hal Foster,
    ed., *Postmodern Culture* (London and Sydney: Pluto Press, 1985), p. 3.
[5] *Ibid.*, p. 9.

tivist paradigm of communicative action, otherwise called the paradigm of understanding. This is based upon the structures of intersubjectivity as implied in the mutual understanding achieved through communicative action. Ever since Hegel the modern subject has been perceived as a problem. Hegel himself tried to overcome the subjectivism of modern philosophy by replacing subject-centred reason with Absolute Knowledge, but conceived as self-consciousness. Even the radical critics of modernity, Nietzsche and Heidegger, remain, according to Habermas, caught in the aporias of the paradigm of consciousness, however much they try to get free. They did not take the one way out, namely the denial of subject-centred reason in favour of reason as communicative action. As Thomas McCarthy sums it up:

Habermas's strategy is to return to the counterdiscourse of modernity – neglected by Nietzsche and his followers – in which the principle of self-sufficient, self-assertive subjectivity was exposed to telling criticism and 'counterreckoning' of the cost of modernity was drawn up. Examining the main crossroads in this counterdiscourse, he points to indications of a path opened but not pursued: the construal of reason in terms of a noncoercive intersubjectivity of mutual understanding and reciprocal recognition.[6]

As Stephen White remarks,[7] Habermas has devoted years to making the communicative paradigm plausible. We have the fruit of his labours in the two large volumes entitled, *The Theory of Communicative Action*.[8]

So far I have not mentioned Michel Foucault, one of the leading figures in the post-modernist debate. Habermas devotes two long chapters to Foucault in *The Philosophical Discourse of Modernity*.[9] There is some difficulty in classifying Foucault's thought, first because it was in a process of constant development right up to his early death at age fifty-seven in

6   In his Introduction to Jürgen Habermas, *The Philosophical Discourse of Modernity* (Cambridge: The Polity Press, 1987), p. xxvi.
7   Stephen K. White, *The Recent Work of Jürgen Habermas: Reason, Justice and Modernity* (Cambridge: Cambridge University Press, 1988), p. 4.
8   Jürgen Habermas, *The Theory of Communicative Action*, vol. 1: *Reason and the Rationalization of Society* (Boston: Beacon Press, 1984); vol. 2: *Lifeworld and System: A Critique of Functionalist Reason* (Boston: Beacon Press, 1987).
9   *The Philosophical Discourse of Modernity*, pp. 238–93.

1984, and second because he claims to be giving a historical account of systems of thought, so that it is not always easy to distinguish his own views from those he is simply narrating.

There is some similarity between his thought and structuralism. He set out to uncover the fundamental cultural codes that as anonymous forms of thought impose order upon experience. However, these underlying codes or conceptual grids were historical systems of thought, subject to mutations when one set of preconceptions gave way to another in an arbitrary fashion. He did not therefore share the structuralist claim to reach the permanent, necessary, universal pattern of the mind. He vehemently repudiated the designation 'structuralist'. In the Foreword to the English edition of *The Order of Things*, he pleaded with the English reader to avoid the misunderstanding he had met with in France. 'In France', he writes, 'certain half-witted "commentators" persist in labelling me a "structuralist". I have been unable to get it into their tiny minds that I have used none of the methods, concepts, or key terms that characterize structural analysis'.[10]

His reaction over-simplifies his relation to structuralism. What he shares with structuralism is the refusal of the hermeneutical search for deeper meaning, a meaning hidden in the depths of subjective interiority to be brought to the surface in interpretation. His critique and decentring of the subject makes Foucault clearly post-modern. What even more clearly makes him post-modern is his recognition of the subtle and unacknowledged relationship between power and truth in any society. With the post-moderns in general, also with feminism, there is admitted the impurity of reason, which is always found mixed (diluted?) with history and tradition, with the body and desire, with interest and power.

A question frequently asked is whether Foucault is concerned with the subject or with power. Towards the end of his life, looking back upon the previous twenty years of his work, he declared that 'it is not power, but the subject, which is the

10   Michel Foucault, *The Order of Things: An Archaeology of the Human Sciences* (New York: Vintage Books, 1973), p. xiv.

general theme of my research'. The goal of his work for the past twenty years was not 'to analyze the phenomena of power, nor to elaborate the foundations of such an analysis'. Instead his objective had been 'to create a history of the different modes by which, in our culture, human beings are made subjects'.[11] Actually, as one writer points out, Foucault has to be concerned with both the subject and power because each element is directly related to the other.[12] The important point to recognize is that he does not regard power as evil.[13] His analyses aim at an understanding of the process through which subjects are formed; and a subject is that which is amenable to the effects of power. It is 'the handle by which power takes a hold of/on individual human beings'.[14]

But this is to consider Foucault's thought from the standpoint of his later writings. It was in the last three volumes of *The History of Sexuality* and in the interviews from the same period that Foucault introduced the famous triangle of knowledge, power and the self and described his work in terms of three ontologies:

Three domains of genealogy are possible. First, an historical ontology of ourselves in relation to truth through which we constitute ourselves as subjects of knowledge; second, an historical ontology of ourselves in relation to a field of power through which we constitute ourselves as subjects acting on others; third, an historical ontology in relation to ethics through which we constitute ourselves as moral agents.[15]

What has happened is that the turn towards the self in the later Foucault has necessitated a re-evaluation of his earlier work. He himself distributes his writing under the three axes of genealogy, genealogy being the study of the emergence and descent of the practices proper to each domain of analysis. All

---

[11] Michel Foucault, 'Afterword: the subject and power', in Hubert L. Dreyfus and Paul Rabinow, *Michel Foucault: Beyond Structuralism and Hermeneutics*, 2nd edn (Chicago: University of Chicago Press, 1983), pp. 208–9.

[12] Karlis Racevskis, 'Michel Foucault, Rameau's nephew, and the question of identity', in *The Final Foucault*, ed. James Bernauer and David Rasmussen, (Cambridge, MA, and London: MIT Press, 1988), p. 23.

[13] See 'The ethic of care for the self as a practice of freedom: an interview with Michel Foucault', in *The Final Foucault*, p. 18.

[14] Racevskis, in *The Final Foucault*, p. 23.

[15] Dreyfus and Rabinow, *Michel Foucault*, p. 237.

three axes were present, he declares, in *Madness and Civilization*: the truth axis in *The Birth of the Clinic* and *The Order of Things*, the power axis in *Discipline and Punish* and the ethical axis in *The History of Sexuality*.[16]

A complaint made against Foucault is that, while attacking modern subjectivity as a distortion and diminution of the human being, he offered nothing in its place. He sought to release human beings from the prison of modern identity, but gave only brief indications or hints of any new kind of subjectivity. But it must be remembered that Foucault's work remained unfinished at his death and that the turn to the subject and the analysis of the ethical dimension are found for the most part in unsystematic form in various interviews he gave. Before piecing together the indications he gives of a new kind of subjectivity, I will outline his critique of the modern subject.

The idea that made Foucault's work notorious was his proclamation of the death of man. He rejoiced in the imminence of that death. 'It is comforting', he wrote in *The Order of Things*, 'however, and a source of profound relief to think that man is only a recent invention, a figure not yet two centuries old, a new wrinkle in our knowledge, and that he will disappear again as soon as that knowledge has discovered a new form'.[17] And then there are the closing sentences of the same work, with their evocative image of the figure in the sand:

As the archaeology of our thought easily shows, man is an invention of recent date. And one perhaps nearing its end.

If those arrangements were to disappear as they appeared, if some event of which we can at the moment do no more than sense the possibility – without knowing either what its form will be or what it promises – were to cause them to crumble, as the ground of Classical thought did, at the end of the eighteenth century, then one can certainly wager that man would be erased, like a face drawn in sand at the edge of the sea.[18]

However, before joining some critics in denouncing this as a pessimistic nihilism, destructive of Western culture, let us

[16] *Ibid.*   [17] *The Order of Things*, p. xxiii.   [18] *Ibid.*, p. 387.

determine more closely its meaning. Note, first, that Foucault uses the term 'man', to designate specifically the modern subject. He keeps the term 'human being' for the wider sense of the subject as transcending the 'man' as fabricated by modernity. We are therefore dealing with a particular conception, belonging to a particular historical epoch. The classical age, which preceded the modern, did not for example know 'man' in the modern sense.

Observe, secondly, that the proclamation of the death of man occurs in *The Order of Things*, which develops its analysis along the axis of truth and thus is concerned with man as the subject of knowledge. In seeing man as a recent invention and one shortly to pass away, Foucault is drawing attention to man as an epistemological subject, namely to man as, not merely the difficult object of knowledge, but also the sovereign subject of knowledge. He is the being through whom that knowledge is attained which renders all knowledge possible. Foucault is attacking modern anthropocentrism, urging us to awaken from our anthropological sleep and pointing to the aporias into which our egocentrism leads.

The modern subject takes on the strange character of an empirico-transcendental doublet. 'As transcendental', summarizes James Bernauer, 'he is constructor of the world, director of the life process, transparent thinker of his own unthought. As empirical, he is like any other object: subject to prediction, to alien forces, to a history which antedates him.'[19] The aporia that implied is expressed well in Dreyfus and Rabinow's book:

At first, philosophers and human scientists became enmeshed in various attempts to ground knowledge by showing that the transcendental and the empirical can be both the same and yet essentially different. But they found that if one reduced man to his empirical side one could not claim scientific objectivity nor account for the obscurity and contingency of man's empirical nature.[20]

There is no need here to follow their analysis further through to

[19] 'The prisons of man: Foucault's negative theology', *International Philosophical Quarterly*, 27 (1987), pp. 365–80.
[20] Dreyfus and Rabinow, *Michel Foucault*, pp. 41–2.

the other doubles created by modern subjectivity and their self-defeating character. Enough has been said to make clear the paradox inherent in the modern conception of the subject.

Can we at this point open up a theological perspective? James Bernauer does so in his article, 'The prisons of man: Foucault's negative theology',[21] and he records two occasions on which Foucault referred to his own work as a negative theology. Let me elaborate this, following Bernauer. The fabrication of the modern subject was a divinization of man. Descartes' *cogito* to which we can trace the origin of the modern subject, transferred to man the function of God as the source of reality and intelligibility. Foucault's anti-humanism, or more precisely anti-modernity, is a negative theology rather than a negative anthropology, because what he is rejecting is yet another conceptualization of God, namely, the rejection of that finite figure who had taken upon himself the role of the Absolute.

To turn now to the second axis in Foucault's genealogical analysis: the axis of power. The declaration of the death of man became for him the starting point of a politics of the self, which would resist the power of our present culture to determine our identity. He was critical of the rational, self-reflective, self-disciplining subject of modernity, because he saw how easily that subject could be drawn into the networks of controlling, normalizing power, characteristic of the modern age. That modern form of power he called in his later writings 'bio-power' – a power that organizes populations for increased productivity, subjugating our bodies and pleasures, according to the norm of a docile body.

In investigating modern identity, Foucault examines two sets of social practices: those of the prison in *Discipline and Punish*[22] and those of sexuality in *The History of Sexuality*.[23] This brings to light a particular form of power and the manner in which it

---

[21] See note 19.

[22] Michel Foucault, *Discipline and Punish: The Birth of the Prison* (New York: Vintage Books, 1979).

[23] Michel Foucault, *The History of Sexuality* I: *An Introduction* (New York: Vintage Books, 1980); II: *The Use of Pleasure* (New York: Vintage Books, 1986); III: *The Care of the Self* (New York: Pantheon, 1986).

operates. That form of power represents a shift from a sovereign and juridical conception of power, exercised in the name of a personal ruler and through law, to a disciplinary and strategic conception.

Disciplinary power is exercised by agents who are themselves products of that power. Teachers and administrators are, for example, made by the educational regime. No one transcends the field of power. It is strategy or control without a strategist or controller. The power is diffuse and all-pervasive but detailed in its application. It is productive, not just repressive. It produces patterns of behaviour, ways of thought, forms of desires and interests. It is universal. The inmates of schools, hospitals and factories are under the same kind of management as the inmates of prisons. They are subjected to rules and training, with an assessment of their behaviour in terms of normality or deviance.

The modern form of power is intimately bound up with knowledge. So much so that we cannot speak of power on the one side and knowledge on the other, but of the various forms of power/knowledge. Knowledge is a technique of power, and no power can be exercised without the extraction, appropriation, distribution or retention of knowledge. Power thus implies the elaboration of a field of knowledge. Knowledge on its part requires a system of communication, which is an exercise of power.

It would be wrong, however, to suppose that Foucault's attitude to power/knowledge was purely negative. In an interview he gave just before he died, he offered some clarification of his thought on power. By relationships of power, he said,

I mean that in human relations, whatever they are – whether it be a question of communicating verbally, as we are doing right now, or a question of a love relationship, an institutional or economic relationship – power is always present: I mean the relationship in which one wishes to direct the behavior of another.

He goes on to say:

One must observe also that there cannot be relations of power unless the subjects are free. If one or the other were completely at the disposition of the other and became his thing, an object on which he can exercise an infinite and unlimited violence, there would not be relations of power. ... This means that in the relations of power, there is necessarily the possibility of resistance – of violent resistance, of escape, of ruse, of strategies that reverse the situation – there would be no relations of power.[24]

Foucault admits that the relationships of power may be unbalanced. His work in general offers a critique of the cognitive and institutional structures of modern life. Much that we regard as enabling is in fact constraining. The question to be answered is how we can weigh degrees of constraint against degrees of enablement.[25]

Foucault does not favour the paradigm of liberation. The drive for emancipation may not be the same as a quest for freedom. Emancipatory action against oppression may be mystifying, hiding the network of normalizing power controlling the subject. In particular, he rejected what he called 'the repressive hypothesis' concerning sexuality, namely, the contention that the history of sexuality is the history of increasing repression from the seventeenth century until its highest point in the Victorian Age. On the contrary, the same period saw an explosion of interest in sex, a proliferation of studies on sex, a multiplication of experts dealing with sex and, in general, incessant discourse about sex. In other words, what we are dealing with is not negative repression, but the deployment of positive, productive forms of disciplinary power, creating norms and a body of recognized knowledge, patterns of thought and behaviour, specific modes of training and education, all serving to control without identifiable repression.

Freedom is not the abolition or destruction of power, but a relationship of permanent provocation; it is the refusal to submit the recalcitrance of the will in the network of power relationships. Foucault takes over a Greek word to describe the relation of the human being in the situation of freedom. 'Rather than speaking of an essential freedom', he writes, 'it would be better to speak of an "agonism" – of a relationship

[24] From 'The ethic care for the self as a practice of freedom: an interview', in *The Final Foucault*, pp. 11–12.
[25] Cf. White, *The Recent Work of Jürgen Habermas*, pp. 144–5.

which is at the same time reciprocal incitation and struggle; less of a face-to-face confrontation which paralyzes both sides than a permanent provocation'.[26] The Greek word means 'a combat'. 'The term would hence imply a physical contest in which the opponents develop a strategy of reaction and of mutual taunting as in a wrestling match'.[27]

With the theme of resistance, struggle, agonism, we are entering into Foucault's genealogy of ethics, the third axis of his genealogical analysis or historical ontology. Here only a few scattered remarks are possible because Foucault died before he finished his project in that area and because his final thoughts are distributed over a comparatively large number of interviews and essays, not all of which I have had access to. A few remarks will, however, enable me to make some concluding reflections about the modern subject on my own account.

Ethics for Foucault is 'the kind of relationship you ought to have with yourself, *rapport à soi* . . . which determines how the individual is supposed to constitute himself as a moral subject of his own actions'.[28] The genealogy of ethics examines how an individual forms that self-relationship that makes one a moral subject. Foucault analyses the various practices by which we attempt to become moral agents. An action is ethical if it contributes to the formation of our subjectivity. Among the actions that do so are sexual practices. Foucault believed that our sexual *rapport à soi* is of primary importance in the constitution of the self.[29]

When the first volume of *The History of Sexuality* was published, it was presented as the first part of a six-volume project on how sexuality became an object of knowledge. However, the research required for the subsequent volumes led him to change the direction of the project, so that the three volumes now published deal with the function of sexuality in self-understanding. He began with the culture of Classical Greece, with

[26] Dreyfus and Rabinow, *Michel Foucault*, p. 222.   [27] *Ibid.* (translator's note).
[28] Dreyfus and Rabinow, *Michel Foucault*, p. 238.
[29] Cf. Deborah Cook, 'The turn towards subjectivity: Michel Foucault's legacy', *Journal of the British Society of Phenomenology*, 18 (1987), p. 218.

its problemization of sexual pleasures. He proceeded to the Greco-Roman culture of the first two centuries of our era, which cultivated a care of the self, aimed at self-making and self-mastery. He thus came to Christianity, which was concerned with purity and self-renunciation.

Foucault finds in Christianity a distinctive technique of the self, namely, the practices of confession and examination of conscience.

Christianity, he writes, requires another form of truth obligation different from faith. Each person has the duty to know who he is, that is, to try to know what is happening inside him, to acknowledge faults, to recognize temptations, to locate desires, and everyone is obliged to disclose these things either to God or to others in the community and hence to bear public or private witness against oneself. The truth obligations of faith and the self are linked together. This link permits a purification of the soul impossible without self-knowledge.[30]

The obligation of disclosing oneself, which made Christianity a confessing religion, was fulfilled in different ways at different times. In Christianity of the first centuries it was carried out by *exomologesis*, namely by a ritual recognizing of oneself as a sinner and penitent. From the fourth century we find *exagoreusis*, that is self-examination as in the Christian monasteries. Then comparatively late on in the thirteenth century, came the sacrament of penance and private confession of sins. But what all these confessing practices did was to make the self a hidden reality, the truth of which had to be uncovered by a process of self-interpretation. 'From that moment on', writes Foucault, 'the self was no longer something to be made but something to be renounced and deciphered'.[31] The pastoral power of the Church, exercised in these confessional practices, is an instance of the normalizing network of disciplinary power. In the eighteenth century the practice of confession, with its endless verbalization of thoughts and desires in a process of self-disclosure, moved outside the Church and became all-perva-

---

[30] Luther H. Martin, Huck Gutman and Patrick H. Hutton, eds., *Technologies of the Self: A Seminar with Michel Foucault* (Amherst: University of Massachusetts Press, 1988), p. 40.

[31] Dreyfus and Rabinow, *Michel Foucault*, p. 248.

sive in our culture. Confession now plays a part in justice, medicine, education, family relations and love relations, in the most ordinary and in the most solemn affairs of life.

If we allow for the difficulty of interpreting the last, incomplete writings of Foucault, we may still, it seems to me, say that Foucault rejected the whole idea that we have a deeper, hidden self, which we have to decipher. He thought that Christianity had caused Western culture to make a wrong move, so that 'the problem of ethics as an aesthetics of existence is covered over by the problem of purification'.[32] He envisioned a more straightforward self-making in which in an aesthetics of existence the principal work of art one has to take care of is one's own life.[33]

When confronted with the intellectual manifestations of post-modernity, philosophers and theologians are tempted to cry out, 'Nihilism'. An understandable, and yet, I think, too hasty a reaction. In discussing Derrida and the deconstructionists in *What is Living, What is Dead in Christianity Today?* I remarked that when faith is not idolatrous, it is difficult to distinguish from nihilism. What does distinguish the negative experience of faith from the unfaith of nihilism is precisely the refusal of closure, a refusal shared by deconstructionism. I went on to formulate the experience of faith in a language that echoed the deconstructionist approach.

Hence the presence of faith is not the immediate presence of a luminous reality or self-authenticating truth but the presence of a hidden God in the darkness or void at the heart of human existence. The epiphany of the hidden God is a centerless repetition of successive reinterpretations, an endless play of significations, which cannot be halted by appeal to a definitive truth or final expression or by a claim to have uncovered the structure of all possible interpretations.[34]

Is it not possible to say something similar when confronted with Foucault's rejection of a deeper self?

For the Christian the experience of the self is inevitably

---

[32] *Ibid.*
[33] For this interpretation of Foucault, see Charles Taylor, 'Foucault on freedom and truth', *Political Theory*, 12 (1984), pp. 179–81.
[34] Charles Davis, *What is Living, What is Dead in Christianity Today?* (San Francisco: Harper & Row, 1986), p. 76.

negative, or at least ambiguous, because the self is the arena for an endless struggle with evil. There can be an idolatry of the 'true self', according to which contingent forms of positive selfhood are given an eternal significance. Those contingent forms thus become prisons, closing the human being off from that movement into the Beyond, which is the experience of transcendence. The relation of oneself to oneself must become a strategy of renunciation to prevent the locking of the self in a prison of the self's own making. As James Bernauer writes:

> This strategy of renunciation enabled Christian experience to avoid the danger of the spiritual death of modern positivist self-identity. For the Christian, the truths of the self were always precarious, for they always related to the soul's continual conflict with the evil within itself. There could be no firm allegiance to a positive self, for there was no truth about the self that could not be utilized by the Evil One as a device for ensnaring the soul. The effect of this continuing self-renunciation was to open the subject's existence to a field of indefinite interpretation, relativizing any particular anthropology.[35]

I am not sure how far this represents Foucault's own thinking, but it is a provocative application of his thought.

In this matter Augustine had a profound but distorting influence. On the one hand, Augustine is the exemplary instance at the beginning of Western culture of the experience of the interior self in that self's relationship with God. He is at the origin of Christian individualism, with its stress upon the dignity of each human person. Western civilization would not be what it has been and is without the contributions of Augustinian inwardness and subjectivity. But on the debit side, Augustine linked the discovery of the inward or interior self with a withdrawal from the world, so that the interior self was in a state of alienation from what lay outside it. That state of alienation extended to the body and its sexuality. The sinful state of fallen humanity is identified with the rebellion of lower appetites against the control of reason, in particular with involuntary, uncontrollable movements of the genital organs. In brief, Augustine combined a self-affirmation of an interior

---

[35] 'The prisons of man: Foucault's negative theology', *International Philosophical Quarterly*, 27 (1987), p. 379.

self with a renunciation of all that lay outside the realm of interiority, including the body and other human beings. Newman's remark about resting 'in the thought of two and two only supreme and luminously self-evident beings, myself and my Creator'[36] is very Augustinian. But I think we need Foucault to remind us that the self is not a self-evident being, any more so than God is.

However, as between Foucault and Habermas, there is a profound philosophical question that demands reflection: what is the ontological reality of intersubjectivity? Or, to put it another way: is there a human ontological reality beyond the individual self? For Kant beyond the autonomous self there was the transcendent order of faith. For Hegel beyond the individual self was the ontological reality of the State, but a reality to be transcended by the order of absolute spirit.[37] For Lonergan intersubjectivity was a simple prolongation of the pre-human on a level that preceded civilization.and emerged again when civilization collapsed. It existed, therefore, below the level of human society and civil community, not beyond the intelligent, rational, responsible individual subject. What lies beyond the rational self-conscious subject is the order of faith and grace. Lonergan here is Kantian in his presuppositions. Habermas on his part continues the Hegelian approach. There is an ontological reality beyond the autonomous subject, but it is not the State. It is communicative action, with the community and lifeworld it creates. So, perhaps the post-modern identity we are seeking is to be found, not in the realm of subjectivity, which we have supposed since the time of Descartes, but in intersubjectivity. But that positive claim would still have to be limited by a negative theology of the community.

[36] *Apologia pro Vita Sua*, Chapter 1.

[37] For this contrast and its theological consequences, see the unpublished dissertation of Roy Darcus, *The Persistence of Kant and Hegel As Theological Models: The Realm of Faith Versus the Realm of Philosophy As the Grounding for the Autonomy of the Human Subject* (Concordia University, Montreal, 1981).

PART IV

The option for the future

CHAPTER 10

What remains of socialism as a moral and religious ideal

In a sense it is impossible to compare socialism and capitalism because they belong to different categories of reality and are thus essentially incomparable. Socialism is a political vision of a moral and religious character. Capitalism on its part is a self-regulating system that has established itself as autonomous in relation to the rest of the social structure. Of itself it deploys a purely functional or means-end rationality, closed to any ethical or religious considerations such as the solidarity of all persons.

Michael Novak in *The Spirit of Democratic Capitalism*[1] has striven to transform capitalism into an ideal, but he can do so only by supposing against the historical evidence that there is an essential relationship between capitalism and democratic and liberal values. The absence of such a relationship has been recently shown again by the flourishing of capitalism under Ronald Reagan, while at the same time 'liberal' became a dirty word.

Again, Novak, unlike many recent defenders of capitalism, recognizes that 'not all human goods and services are appropriately assigned to markets'. He allows that there should be 'welfare provisions for those too young, too old, disabled, afflicted with illness or nervous disorder, etc., and unable to be self-reliant'.[2]

I agree with those who find that qualification inconsistent

---

[1] Michael Novak, *The Spirit of Democratic Capitalism* (New York: American Enterprise Institute/Simon & Schuster Publications, 1982).
[2] Michael Novak, *Will It Liberate? Questions About Liberation Theology* (New York: Paulist Press, 1986), p. 215.

with the principle of capitalism as a self-regulating market system. But it is none the worse for that. Implicitly it points us towards a development in the concept of the State and a rejection of the alternative: capitalism or a centrally planned economy.

There have been a number of political and economic regimes that have called themselves socialist. None of them has proved satisfactory. There is, in any case, no clearly distinguishable system that can claim the epithet 'socialist'. The reason is not confused thinking, as Novak would have it, but that the contribution of socialism lies elsewhere. It is time to elaborate that by considering socialism in its authentic form as a political vision with a moral and religious content.

Barbara Taylor in her study of socialism and feminism in the nineteenth century writes in this fashion about political visions:

Political visions are fragile. They appear – and are lost again. Ideas formulated in one generation are frequently forgotten, or repressed, by the next; goals which seemed necessary and realistic to progressive thinkers of one era are shelved as visionary and utopian by their successors. Aspirations which find voice in certain periods of radical endeavour are stifled, or even wholly silenced, in others. The history of all progressive movements is littered with such half-remembered hopes with dreams that have failed.[3]

Fragile though they are, political visions are essential to the health of a society. They prevent politics becoming mere business motivated by a cynical self-interest. It is a major objection to neo-conservatives that they deal crudely and harshly with a noble ideal. They do so at a time when we are short on social vision and acutely aware of the fragility and – worse – the corruptibility of our social ideals. To indulge in dreams is not our present temptation. The temptation is rather to settle for a cynical realism with its sole criterion of immediate success.

The ideal that Novak dismisses in *The Spirit of Democratic Capitalism* and his other writings is socialism. But socialism is

---

[3] Barbara Taylor, *Eve and the New Jerusalem: Socialism and Feminism in the Nineteenth Century* (London: Virago, 1983), p. ix.

not just a dream that failed. Kolakowski is an ex-Marxist, who now dubs Marxism 'the greatest fantasy of our century'.[4] Yet he writes:

Are we fools to try to keep thinking in socialist terms? I do not think so. Whatever has been done in Western Europe to bring about more justice, more security, more educational opportunity, more welfare and more state responsibility for the poor and helpless, could never have been achieved without the pressure of socialist ideologies and socialist movements, for all their naiveties and illusions.[5]

Let me gloss that in this way: capitalism was basically unsound in so far as it required socialist pressure to be just; socialism, despite its harmful simplicities, was basically sound inasmuch as it provided that pressure.

But, surely, if Novak tramples down the socialist ideal, he does so in the name of another ideal: that of democratic capitalism. Novak, it may be urged, is concerned first and foremost with ideals, not with history or facts. Not with reinterpreting the past, but with 'trying to understand within the present those institutional ideals and systemic sources by which a better future may be shaped'.[6] Not with passing judgement on the practice of capitalism but with grasping the ideals latent in its practice.[7] And he declares, perhaps a little querulously: 'If it is legitimate for socialists to dream and to state their ideals, it is also legitimate for democratic capitalists to dream and to state our ideals'.[8]

However, does democratic capitalism as presented by Novak take off as an ideal? It seems to me to be too closely tied to the criterion of measurable success to function as an ideal or moral vision. Novak explains his own change from socialism to capitalism as motivated by the realization that an unworkable ideal, far from being morally superior, is a false ideal because it

4 Leszek Kolakowski, *Main Currents of Marxism: Its Origin, Growth, and Dissolution. III: The Breakdown* (Oxford: Clarendon Press, 1978), p. 523.
5 Leszek Kolakowski and Stuart Hampshire, eds., *The Socialist Idea: A Reappraisal* (New York: Basic Books, 1974), p. 16.
6 Novak, *The Spirit of Democratic Capitalism*, pp. 27–8.   7 *Ibid.*, pp. 358–9.
8 *Ibid.*, p. 359.

is out of touch with human reality.[9] Socialism does not work, capitalism does and is therefore more acceptable, even morally. But workable in relation to what? When Novak insists that democratic capitalism is not the Kingdom of God and is not without sin[10] is he talking of capitalism as a historical fact or as a moral vision? If as a historical fact, then no higher claim would seem to be justified than that, in Novak's own words, 'all other known systems of political economy are worse'.[11] Now even if we allow that socialists have not been able to devise a more workable economic system than capitalism, that does not make capitalism acceptable. One might note with Peter Berger – no friend to socialism – that empirical reality does not exactly correspond to capitalism or socialism, that there is no such thing as pure capitalism or pure socialism, and that, while the human race has shown enormous imagination in thinking up different arrangements, as with kinship institutions, 'it has been rather unimaginative about economic systems. Most of them are modifications of those two ideas.'[12] In other words, if we are talking about historical fact and present reality and are engaged in trying to make our economic system more work-able in terms of the common good than it has been or is, then we have to go beyond a simple-minded dichotomy between capitalism and socialism and recognize that any successful arrangement will not fit comfortably under either heading. However, if Novak, in admitting that capitalism does not measure up to the full standards of the Kingdom, is talking of capitalism as an ideal he is selling Christians short in the market of ideals.

Because the Kingdom of God can never be identified with any political order actually achieved on earth does not mean that the Kingdom is not the ideal and standard for Christians in their political activity. Christians should not settle for less as their ultimate goal or guiding vision. It is a mistaken other worldliness or moral dualism to regard the Kingdom as a

---

[9] *Ibid.*, p. 198.   [10] *Ibid.*, pp. 28 and 359.   [11] *Ibid.*, p. 28.
[12] Peter Berger, 'Capitalism and socialism: empirical facts', in *Capitalism and Socialism: A Theological Inquiry*, ed. Michael Novak (Washington, DC: American Enterprise Institute for Public Policy Research, 1978), p. 85.

promise for the future, a reward in the hereafter for enduring this vale of tears, but as unworkable for the present. Its final fulfilment may be beyond history, the contours of its active presence within history may be hidden from us, but that does not entitle Christians, who share it as a vision, to dismiss any of its demands as unworkable. Our age – and every other age for that matter – is a moral shambles. That does not justify us in tailoring our moral vision to what our contemporaries consider feasible. The eschatological character of the Kingdom does not mean that we may with easy conscience omit it from the equation of present policy as unrealistic; it does mean that repeated failure to embody our vision of redeemed humanity cannot destroy our hope or lessen our striving, because we are assured of final victory.

To a degree, Novak recognizes that Christians cannot lower their standards or limit their ideals. In the same paragraph in which he admits that democratic capitalism does not measure up to the full standards of the Christian vision of the Kingdom, he declares that democratic capitalism welcomes 'judgement under that Kingdom's clear light'.[13] But there is a confusion here between fact and ideal. As an ideal, democratic capitalism should measure up to the full standards of the Kingdom; as a fact or particular achievement, it will always fall short. But the defects of our moral achievement do not justify us in limiting our moral vision or ideal.

It is my contention that the ideal of democratic capitalism as presented by Novak and others is in effect a narrowing of the Christian vision. It includes a large element of moral cynicism. Further, for me the troubling future of our present culture is not its alleged anti-capitalism, which is seen as undermining our liberties, but its disillusionment with socialism, a disillusionment that is leading to apathy and the death of social idealism.

Let me show the narrowing of the Christian vision by contrasting Novak's basic approach with that of Matthew Lamb in his book *Solidarity with Victims: Toward a Theology of*

---

[13] Novak, *The Spirit of Democratic Capitalism*, p. 359.

Social Transformation (New York: Crossroad, 1982). 'No elite on earth has been without its victims' remarks Novak. So, unfortunate, but there you are. There must be victims, but we must reconcile ourselves to their fate. This resigned acceptance of the human cost makes one pause before the later eulogy of the spirit of democratic capitalism. When Novak writes 'The spirit of democratic capitalism is the spirit of development, risk, experiment, adventure. It surrenders present security for future betterment',[14] one cannot but ask: whose security is surrendered? Whose future betterment is ensured? The history of capitalism makes one question whether the group that suffers and the group that gains are the same. How does Novak justify the human cost? His thesis is summed up in the second half of the sentence I have already quoted. To give the sentence in full: 'No elite on earth has been without its victims, but not all have equally liberated and enriched the many'.[15] In other words, capitalism delivers the goods and does so by liberating the productive energies of individual and private groups. What we are offered is a utilitarian ethic, built on the presuppositions of liberal individualism. Lost are the paradox and transcendence of the Christian social vision. The very title of Lamb's book, *Solidarity with Victims*, indicates a contrasting approach. Lamb expresses his aim in terms generally acceptable to practitioners of political and liberation theologies. He writes: 'This book tries to discern the outlines of a practice of reason and of religion in a self-critical solidarity with the victims of history'.[16] To give a longer quotation:

Vox victimarum vox dei – the cries of victims are the voice of God. The scandal of the cross is the scandal of God identified with all the victims of history in the passion of Christ. That identification was not a passive acceptance of suffering but an empowering transformation whereby the forces of death and evil were overcome through the resurrection. This empowering transformation was not an isolated, individual event cut off from the rest of human history. It was an event the meaning of which challenges those who believe to engage in

---

[14] *Ibid.*, p. 48.   [15] *Ibid.*, p. 27.
[16] Matthew L. Lamb, *Solidarity With Victims: Toward a Theology of Social Transformation* (New York: Crossroad, 1982), p. xiii.

a discipleship of faith, hope and love. The discipleship is a life lived in a dying identification with the victims.[17]

In the Christian vision, the victims are not the unfortunate byproduct of the onward march of human society towards affluence and individual freedom, but the place in society where we meet both the judgement and the redemption of God. To borrow words from Horkheimer, 'theology is the hope that injustice does not have the last word, the longing that the murderer may not triumph over his victim'.[18]

Why is it, then, that many Christians have found it possible to speak of Christian socialism without a sense of incongruity, whereas the phrase 'Christian capitalism' has the impact of an oxymoron? Is it, as Novak suggests, that supporters of capitalism have neglected to articulate their ideals, so that the reputation for moral idealism has gone by default and wrongly to socialism? Is it, Schumpeter, Berger and Novak argue,[19] that in its economic success capitalism undermines itself culturally by creating a new class of intellectuals, with a vested interest in criticism and social unrest? Or is it, as Benne explains, due to a superficial resemblance between socialist rhetoric and Christian values? Benne writes:

One obvious reason is that the rhetoric of socialism contains many close parallels to deeply embedded values in Judeo-Christian tradition. Moral rhetoric is very close to the surface in the *theory* of socialism whereas the moral values of democratic capitalism are much less visible, at least in its theoretical foundations. The convergence of value systems in the traditions of socialism and Judeo-Christian humanism is readily grasped; the case for democratic capitalism is much more subtle and complex.[20]

But all these are excuses. The basic reason why Christian capitalism, unlike Christian socialism, smacks of contradiction is that capitalism requires the acceptance of systemic or struc-

[17] *Ibid.*, p. 1.
[18] Max Horkheimer, *Die Sehnsucht nach dem ganz Anderen: Ein Interview mit Kommentar von Helmut Gumnior* (Hamburg: Furche, 1975), pp. 61–2.
[19] See the references to Schumpeter and Berger in Robert Benne, *The Ethic of Democratic Capitalism: A Moral Reassessment* (Philadelphia: Fortress, 1981), pp. 5–16, Novak, *The Spirit of Democratic Capitalism*, pp. 182–6.
[20] Benne, *The Ethic of Democratic Capitalism*, p. 11.

tural injustice in the name of economic success and individualist freedom.

Hence, the acceptance of capitalism as an ideal demands a
fair dose of moral cynicism. This is covered over in different
ways. Berger grants that it is almost impossible not to sympath-
ize with the socialist vision of a restored community, but then
states bluntly that it cannot be realized in the modern world.
Socialism is a contradictory attempt to combine modernizing
and counter-modernizing themes or to have modernization
without the cost or loss of community.[21] Novak speaks of the
sense of sin fostered by democratic capitalism, and then takes
flight poetically in comparing the destruction of community
brought about by capitalism to the mystical dark night of the
soul:

The 'wasteland' at the heart of democratic capitalism is like a field of
battle, on which individuals wander alone, in some confusion amid
many casualties. Nonetheless, like the dark night of the soul in the
inner journey of the mystics, this desert has an indispensable purpose.
It is maintained out of respect for the diversity of human consciences,
perceptions, and intentions. It is swept clean out of reverence for the
sphere of the transcendent to which the individual has access through
the self, beyond the mediations of social institutions.[22]

Thus, we are asked to believe that the destruction of human
community by capitalism and its reduction of society to a
collection of homogenized, competing units are due to its
reverence for the Transcendent. That certainly outbids the
socialists. But Novak is unusually deaf to the discords of his own
rhetoric. How else could he have penned these words in his
booklet, *Toward a Theology of the Corporation*?

For many years one of my favorite texts in scripture has been Isaiah
53: 2–3: 'He hath no form nor comeliness; and when we shall see him,
there is no beauty that we should desire him. He is despised and
rejected of men; a man of sorrows and acquainted with grief; he was
despised and we esteemed him not.' I would like to apply these words

[21] Berger, 'Capitalism and socialism', p. 98 and as quoted in Benne, *The Ethic of Democratic Capitalism*, p. 13.
[22] Novak, *The Spirit of Democratic Capitalism*, pp. 54–5.

to the modern business corporation, a much despised incarnation of God's presence in this world.[23]

Novak will forgive me if I cannot but think that to compare the modern business corporation to Jesus Christ as Suffering Servant is to make a claim for capitalism that goes beyond the wildest dreams of any socialist.

But to return to the question of moral cynicism. In one way or another, we are asked to reconcile ourselves to the social wasteland produced by capitalism and to the structural injustice of the capitalist system, because the benefits outweigh the cost, because sin makes such injustice inevitable, because modernization with its industrial technology is impossible without the destruction of community, because only capitalism as an economic system is compatible with democracy. The last point is the key theme in Novak's principal book, with its constant reference to *democratic capitalism*. However, historically, there was no essential link between democracy and capitalism. The transition from liberal capitalism to liberal democracy was a difficult one. I am thinking not only of the history of the granting of the vote but of the painful struggle of workers for the basic freedom of association. Nor does present political reality indicate an essential link between capitalism and democracy. Wherever capitalists feel themselves threatened by any attempts consistently to realize and extend liberal, democratic values, they ditch freedom and resort to naked oppression.

What united the Christian socialists was their refusal to come to terms morally with a system they perceived as inhuman and unjust. The points they made were chiefly three: first, that the existing situation was intolerable; second, that the social and economic system must not be disengaged from morality, but must be brought back under moral laws; third, that society must be built upon co-operation not competition.

Thus, Scott Holland declared that two 'deep convictions' should motivate Christians involved in social action. This is how he states them:

[23] Michael Novak, *Toward a Theology of the Corporation* (Washington and London: American Enterprise Institute for Public Policy Research, 1981), p. 33.

First, the present situation is intolerable. And second its solution must be found in the unfaltering assertion of moral, as supreme over mechanical laws.[24]

The first conviction represents the prophetic element in Christian socialism: the refusal to accept any excuse for inaction in the face of injustice. Injustice must be denounced prophetically, not merely in words but in deeds. No arguments to the effect that the negative consequences of the capitalist system are inevitable and must be tolerated for the benefits it brings can be used to justify a passive acceptance of social injustice.

The second conviction, as formulated by Scott Holland, attacks the typical capitalist argument against any interference in economic activity in the name of social reform, namely, that economic laws must be respected. The capitalist assumption here is that economic activity must proceed according to a purely functional or calculative rationality, disengaged from moral or religious considerations. The assumption is a reflection of the historical process whereby the economic order became autonomous, as disengaged not simply from government control but from the traditional moral order. Now the deep conviction of the Christian socialist was, to put it in my own words, that to regard economic activity as subject to a purely calculative or functional rationality, geared simply to economic success, is incompatible with a Christian ethic. Socialism from that standpoint was seen as the reassertion of morality in the economic sphere.

Novak himself, while insisting upon the independence of the political, economic and moral–cultural systems, recognizes that the moral–cultural system is the *sine qua non* of both the political and economic systems.[25] Where, however, he is unconvincing is in supposing that capitalism historically or at present respects the relationship he has drawn. The truth would rather seem to be that capitalism has gradually proved destructive of even the bourgeois liberal ideals with which it was originally associated

[24] Quoted in Bernard Murchland, *The Dream of Christian Socialism: An Essay on Its European Origins* (Washington and London: American Enterprise Institute for Public Policy Research, 1982), p. 15.
[25] Novak, *The Spirit of Democratic Capitalism*, pp. 56–7.

and this largely because it refused to consider human economic activity according to the communicative or moral rationality appropriate to it as human *praxis*, and insisted on interpreting it 'mechanically', that is according to a merely functional rationality. The Christian socialists were right in seeing that assumption as basically unChristian.

In regard to the third point, that society must be built on co-operation not competition, the Christian socialists opposed socialism to individualism. Their concept of socialism is well expressed by Westcott:

Individualism and Socialism correspond with opposite views of humanity. Individualism regards humanity as made up of disconnected or warring atoms; Socialism regards it as an organic whole, a vital unity formed by the combination of contributory members mutually interdependent. It follows that Socialism differs from Individualism both in method and in aim. The method of Socialism is cooperation, the method of individualism is competition. The one regards man as working with man for a common end, the other regards man as working against man for private gain. The aim of Socialism is the fulfillment of service. The aim of Individualism is the attainment of some personal advantage, riches, or place, or fame. Socialism seeks such an organization of life as shall secure for everyone the most complete development of his powers; Individualism seeks primarily the satisfaction of the particular wants of each one in the hope that the pursuit of private interest will in the end secure public welfare.[26]

I do not think that the reaction of the Christian socialists can be dismissed as pious highmindedness nor as an unwarranted assumption of moral superiority. It represents a genuine moral response to capitalist society as they experience it. At the same time, after the analysis of Marx and the historical researches of Lichtheim, Thompson and others, we are in a better position to form a more precise concept of socialism and thus focus more sharply our ethical response.

Historically, socialism was not just a protest against the poverty and misery that accompanied the industrial revolution. It was not primarily a protest against poverty, but a movement for a new social order. Its adherents were character-

[26] Quoted in Murchland, *The Dream of Christian Socialism*, pp. 14–15.

istically from the so-called aristocracy of labour, the better-off, skilled workers. Equality not poverty was the issue. Further, unlike other Romantic reactions to industrial civilization, socialism did not advocate a return to a pre-industrial society. It joined in the drive towards modernization, welcomed science and technology, accepted the Enlightenment view of human beings as free agents capable of making and transforming their world and building a better society in the future. What, then, did they refuse? They refused the reduction of the worker as producer to a wage-earner without any share in the ownership or control of the means of production and therefore compelled to work for the benefit of the capitalist. They rejected the identification of industrialism with capitalism and looked for a co-operative social order, in which labour would no longer be a mere commodity and what was considered the exploitative wage-relationship would be abolished. Lichtheim writes:

The term 'socialism' was originally coined for the purpose of designating a society in which the producers own their tools. Since under modern industrial conditions this cannot be done individually . . . the only reasonable description of socialism is one that centres on common or social ownership. The distinction between state property and social ownership ought to be obvious: the former vests effective control in a political bureaucracy, the latter does not.[27]

Socialism, therefore, should not be identified with state ownership and central planning. To so identify them is not historically accurate. Think, for example, of the debate in Britain between the Fabians who favoured collectivist solutions and the Guild Socialists who argued for a pluralist approach. But what is essential to socialism is the rejection of the wage-relationship, rooted as that is in the fact that wage- and salary-earners do not own the means of production. As Lichtheim says: 'Anything that falls short of abolishing the wage relation has no claim to being described as socialism, although it may be a station of the way thereto'.[28]

The precise moral question raised by capitalism is not, then,

[27] George Lichtheim, *A Short History of Socialism* (New York and Washington: Praeger, 1970), p. 318.
[28] *Ibid.*, p. 317.

the inadequacy of wages or bad conditions of work or the use of power at home or abroad to force concessions one-sidedly in favour of the capitalist. All these objections and others like them may be regarded as abuses of capitalism, capable of removal while leaving the system itself intact. The essential question is whether a social order is just in which the majority of people have no share in the ownership of the means of production and are compelled for their livelihood to sell their labour as a commodity in the market. The socialist case is that such a social order is a routinized disorder, violating the dignity, freedom, solidarity and essential equality of human beings. By its very structure it perpetuates and exacerbates existing inequalities. Because the means of production are in the possession of individuals and corporations who have to make a profit to stay in business, production is not geared to social needs but to the satisfaction of the inessential demand of those who already have purchasing power. Economic growth and technical progress directly benefit the owners, individual and corporate, who claim the profits and only in a roundabout fashion the wage-earners. Even when these are affluent, their lives are at the mercy of the fluctuations of a market responsive only to economic calculation directed to the benefit of the capitalist owners. While labour laws and welfare benefits by the State may offset the worst effects of the system, it does not remove its structural injustice. Socialists want a social order that is integrally human and just. In brief, 'socialism is not about distribution but human relationships – the right distribution is necessary to and made possible by the right relationships but it is morally of subordinate importance'.[29]

Socialism is an ideal. I grant that it is not immediately realizable. That does not make it a false ideal or illusion. A society free from slavery was an ideal governing individual action and social policy long before it was achievable in reality. What postponed the achievement of socialism is that it requires the sacrifice of short-term chiefly economic gains for long-term chiefly non-economic benefits on the part of those moderately

[29] Brian Barry, *The Liberal Theory of Justice: A Critical Examination of the Principal Doctrines in A Theory of Justice by John Rawls* (Oxford: Clarendon Press, 1975), p. 168.

well placed in society. It is a sacrifice understandably hard to ask for and to get as long as there is economic scarcity or insecurity. Further, I admit that as an ideal, socialism requires more careful elaboration particularly in regard to the question of the State and the relationship between socialism and democratic political values.[30] But those admissions do not destroy socialism as a guiding vision. I myself do not feel tempted to replace it by capitalism as an ideal. What Novak, in my opinion, has done is not to establish the capitalist system as an ideal, but to cover it in the borrowed cloak of democracy and bedeck it with theological jewels which like the cloak do not belong to it.

Peter Berger remarks that 'the basic *cultural* fact in Western societies, leaving aside the Third World and those societies that consider themselves socialist, is that capitalism is under assault'.[31] He goes on to speak of the anti-capitalist mood of the intellectual élites of the Western world.[32] Is that a correct reading? Others, including Novak and Benne, would have it so. We may turn to the socialist commentator E. P. Thompson for a different reading.[33] He speaks of the apathy prevalent today. The basic feature of our culture is not a rebellious rejection of the capitalist system but a deep disillusionment with socialism leading to an apathetic conformity to the status quo. One may add here a reference to the recent spread of neo-conservatism. People have rightly recoiled from the harsh reality of communist regimes. If socialism is identified with the kind of regimes imposed on Eastern Europe, then it should be rejected. We rightly rejoice in the recent rebellion of Eastern Europe against those regimes. But the disenchantment with communism has led in the West to a loss of social idealism and a cynical conformity to things as they are. If the number of unemployed is high, the majority of workers are still employed and people fear and resist any proposal for social reform that would call for the subordination of their security and self-interest to the

---

[30] See the admission of E. P. Thompson, *The Poverty of Theory & Other Essays* (New York and London: Monthly Review Press, 1978), p. 367.
[31] Berger, 'Capitalism and socialism', p. 86 (Berger's italics).
[32] *Ibid.*   [33] *The Poverty of Theory*, pp. 213–14.

common good. We are not suffering from an overdose of an unreal idealism, but from a morally apathetic and fearful seeking for a safe niche in our present predatory society. I come back to my initial complaint against Novak. At a time when we are full of disillusionment and short on social vision, he denigrates what has been the chief vehicle of social idealism since the nineteenth century, for Christians as well as for others, and offers in its stead an ideal which is nothing more than a heavily sanitized version of the status quo.

CHAPTER II

Communicative rationality and the grounding of religious hope

A distinctive, recurrent theme of Christian theology today is that of hope. It is a constitutive feature of Latin American Liberation Theology, which, as in the title of Ruben Alves's classic study, can be designated *A Theology of Human Hope*.[1] As for German political theology, one of its chief exponents, Jürgen Moltmann, gave it the programmatic title, *Theology of Hope*;[2] and hope is such a prominent theme in the theology of its other representative, Johann Baptist Metz, that a study of his thought is entitled *Christliche Hoffnung und menschlicher Fortschritt*.[3]

Both Moltmann and Metz have been influenced by Bloch more than by the older Frankfurt School, as represented by Horkheimer and Adorno or by Jürgen Habermas. Ernst Bloch's *Das Prinzip Hoffnung* has had a much greater impact upon theologians than upon Marxists, even of the Western variety. Its influence upon German political theology has been profound and decisive.[4] Outside theological circles Bloch's thought is scarcely treated even with respect. Kolakowski dubs his work 'a futuristic gnosis' and writes contemptuously: 'Certainly at times the reader feels as though he were amid the fumes of an alchemist's laboratory, and when he reduces the

---

[1] Ruben A. Alves, *A Theology of Human Hope* (St Meinrad, IN: Abbey Press, 1972).
[2] Jürgen Moltmann, *Theology of Hope: On the Ground and the Implications of a Christian Eschatology* (New York: Harper & Row, 1965).
[3] Gerhard Bauer, *Christliche Hoffnung und menschlicher Fortschritt: Die politische Theologie von J. B. Metz* (Mainz: Grünewald, 1976).
[4] Cf. *Ibid.*, pp. 113–19. See also the contributions of Moltmann, Metz and Pannenberg to the Bloch *Festschrift, Ernst Bloch zu Ehren: Beiträge zu seinem Werk*, ed. Siegfried Unseld (Frankfurt: Suhrkamp Verlag, 1965).

poetic verbiage to everyday terms he may find it sterile and commonplace'.[5] One would hardly expect Horkheimer and Adorno as critical theorists to be much taken with Bloch's work, because their thought is more aptly called a philosophy of despair than a philosophy of hope.

What about Habermas? He, too, refers to Bloch as agnostic,[6] but also more respectfully as a Marxist Schelling.[7] (It should be remembered that Habermas wrote his doctoral thesis on Schelling.) Nevertheless, a rejection is implied in the designation. Habermas does not agree with Bloch's (and Schelling's) speculative naturalism, the appeal to a *natura naturans* and a doctrine of potency. He, therefore, refuses Bloch's leap into hope beyond the sociological–historical analysis of the objective possibilities in the dialectic of the social process. All the same, he turns away from the philosophy of despair. As Agnes Heller remarks with a reference to his treatment of Adorno and Schelsky in *Legitimation Crisis*,[8] his judgement is that the philosophy of despair is not binding. For that reason he can make his own the motto of Bloch: 'Reason cannot bloom without hope, hope cannot speak without reason, both in a Marxist unity – all other science has no future, all other future no science'.[9]

Habermas, however, as Heller interprets him, has turned away from the philosophy of both hope and despair. Consequently, according to her: 'the lack of the sensuous experiences of hope and despair, of venture and humiliation, is discernible in the structure of his theory: the creature-like aspects of human beings are missing'.[10] A little further on in the same text, she expresses the same point even more strongly:

[5] Leszek Kolakowski, *Main Currents of Marxism: Its Origin, Growth, and Dissolution. Volume 3: The Breakdown* (Oxford: Clarendon Press, 1978), pp. 421–2.
[6] Jürgen Habermas, *Philosophical-Political Profiles*, transl. Frederick G. Lawrence (Cambridge, MA: MIT Press, 1983), p. 73.
[7] The essay on Bloch in *Philosophical-Political Profiles* is entitled 'Ernst Bloch: a Marxist Schelling'.
[8] Jürgen Habermas, *Legitimation Crisis* (London: Heinemann, 1976), especially pp. 125–8.
[9] Quoted at the beginning of the essay on Bloch in *Philosophical-Political Profiles*, p. 61.
[10] Agnes Heller, 'Habermas and Marxism', in *Habermas: Critical Debates*, ed. John B. Thompson and David Held (London: Macmillan, 1982), p. 21.

Habermasian man has, however, no body, no feelings; the 'structure of personality' is identified with cognition, language and interaction. Although Habermas accepts the Aristotelian differentiation between 'life' and 'the good life', one gets the impression that the good life consists solely of rational communication and that needs can be argued for without being felt.[11]

In other words, is reason, even communicative reason, enough for hope? Reason must find its motivation in an attitude of hope. But does not hope to justify itself require anchoring in reason? However, if reason needs hope and hope needs reason, are not both reason and hope floating free without a basis? To affirm so may perhaps be saying the same as Habermas himself when he asserts, 'Both *revolutionary self-confidence* and *theoretical self-certainty* are gone . . .'.[12]

At this point what is necessary is an analysis of hope. Then the question of the possible grounding of hope in communicative rationality may be investigated.[13]

Hope is multi-dimensional. In its full complexity it includes intellectual, volitional and emotional factors. Hope is therefore best seen as an attitude, that is, a set of disposition of the total person. It is a stance taken up towards experience and reality. Let us consider the different factors in turn.

The affective or emotional element in hope precedes, accompanies and follows upon the intellectual affirmations relevant to hope and the decisions and actions that belong to hope. This is the bodily, sensuous, feeling component, which Heller finds lacking in Habermas. Although emotional responses may vary according to purely individual factors, the affective element of hope is rooted in universal features of the human situation. The feeling component of hope is a feel for the world as it is and for human beings as they are. Hope in that way is revelatory of objective reality.

---

[11]   *Ibid.*, p. 22.

[12]   Jürgen Habermas, 'A reply to my critics', in Thompson and Held, *Habermas: Critical Debates*, p. 222 (Habermas's italics).

[13]   Although the synthesis is my own, I have for the account of hope drawn chiefly upon: Donald Evans, *Struggle and Fulfillment: The Inner Dynamics of Religion and Morality* (Cleveland and London: Collins, 1979); John Macquarrie, *Christian Hope* (New York: Seabury, 1978); Nicholas Lash, *A Matter of Hope: A Theologian's Reflections on the Thought of Karl Marx* (London: Darton, Longman & Todd, 1981).

Bloch saw hunger as the elemental energy of hope. For him hunger, not libido, was the fundamental drive. But human hunger opened out on to higher levels than physical hunger. As Habermas summarizes Bloch:

The ever-renewed hunger drives people about, sets the tone for self-preservation as self-expression and, in its enlightened figure, is transformed into an explosive force against the prisons of deprivation in general. This learned hunger, another form of the *docta spes*, develops to the point of a resolution to eliminate all relationships under which people live as forgotten beings.[14]

Hope as hunger is an expression of human finiteness, of human limits. It belongs to what Heller calls 'the creature-like aspects of human beings'.[15] We confront an unknown and unknowable future with trust. Why do we hope rather than despair? Because of the assurance we have received from past experiences. That is only a partial, not a total answer, because the struggle between hope and despair is not just between two people or groups of different temperament, but a struggle within each of us. How can we justify our yielding to hope, instead of succumbing to despair? Even more pressing is the need to justify expanding the force of hope from a drive for self-preservation to an energy of revolutionary self-confidence, directed to emancipation.

Those questions concerning hope as affectivity cannot be answered until we have examined the other elements of hope; and, first, its cognitive element.

The attitude of hope presupposes that we affirm as true some statements about ourselves and the world in which we live; it is, then, constituted in its cognitive dimension by some further affirmations. It presupposes that the world, including human beings, is neither utterly evil nor completely good, but a mixture of good and evil. There would be no place for hope in an irremediably evil universe nor in a universe that could not be bettered. Likewise, there would be no room for hope in a universe of unresolvable absurdity nor in one where the meaning was dazzlingly clear. Hope requires a world and a

[14] *Philosophical-Political Profiles*, p. 61.
[15] Thompson and Held, *Habermas: Critical Debates*, p. 21.

human existence with an openness of texture allowing substantial change. It also demands an ambiguity in the meaning of cosmic and human reality, so that there is no immanent source of certitude for a meaningful future. The Scholastics designated the object of hope as a *bonum arduum*, or difficult good. In other words, the obstacles to reaching that good are so great that its attainment is put into question. How far that question is removed and what removes it concerns the very essence of hope.

Before we ask about that essence, there is one further presupposition of hope to be mentioned: the freedom of human agency. That is presupposed by the volitional element in hope. There can be no hope in a deterministic view of human existence and action, and therefore it is part of the cognitive factor in hope to affirm human freedom.

So far I have spoken of the affirmations concerning the world and human beings presupposed by hope. But what affirmations constitute the cognitive element in the very essence of hope? There are two, it seems to me. Those who live and act in hope have to affirm the objective possibility of what they hope for in turning to the future. For a possibility to be objective it must be rooted in the reality of the past and the present. To be thus rooted is what distinguished genuine hope from utopian illusion. Most writers on hope recognize that. Thus, Ruben Alves writes:

For the sake of hope and human liberation it is therefore of the utmost importance to unmask the pseudo-hopes, visions of the future that are not derived from the reading of the objective movement of the politics of freedom in history. Visions of the future not extracted from history or which do not take the movement of freedom as their basis, cannot be called hope: they are forms of alienation, illusions which cannot inform history because of their unrelatedness to the way of operation of freedom in the world.[16]

Again, Macquarrie writes:

I am saying then that hope has to be related to the present and the past if it is to be saved from irrelevance, escapism and at the worst, the possibility of downright inhumanity. Hope has its being in the tension

---

[16] Alves, *A Theology of Human Hope*, p. 102.

of future and present, driving us out of the present, yet seeing the future from the present situation. A hope that relates only to an imagined future, whether that hope be religious or secular, is a false and alienating hope.[17]

It is therefore essential to hope to affirm that inherent in the past and present human situation is the possibility of what is hoped for. However, for there to be hope it is not enough to affirm a possibility. A second affirmation, an affirmation concerning future actuality, is essential to hope. Somehow hope has to bridge the gap between the possibility and the attainment of a meaningful and liberated human existence. Before we consider what can ground the transition from affirming a possibility to affirming its future realization, we must turn to the third and last element of hope, namely, the volitional.

Hope is the chosen stance of a free agent and the actions that flow from that stance. The stance chosen by those who hope is that of a basic trust in reality, motivating a patient and tenacious pursuit of the good, despite all set-backs and failures. The stance of a confident openness to reality and trust in the future is not the result of a single act of choice, but a disposition gradually formed by a persistent striving for human betterment and fulfilment against obstacles. It presupposes, as we have seen, a conviction that our actions do make a difference, that the overcoming of evil and the achievement of good is at least in part something that can and should be done by our free actions as responsible agents. The volitional element of hope, in so far as it concerns a permanent disposition of the will rather than a single choice, merges with the emotional or affective element with its bodily basis.

In sum, hope is a multi-dimensional attitude, consisting (1) in an enduring disposition of the will to confront the future with confidence despite the negativities of human existence, having (2) an emotional and bodily counterpart and (3) demanding two affirmations at its cognitive core, namely, the affirmation of the objective possibility and the affirmation of the future actuality of a fulfilled human life.

[17] Macquarrie, *Christian Hope*, p. 28.

Is such a hope rational? I want to pursue an answer to that question in the context of Habermas's theory of communicative action and communicative rationality; in other words, while rejecting the Cartesian paradigm of the solitary thinker and the epistemological or subject–object model of knowledge.

Communicative action is action directed towards reaching an understanding among people trying to come to an agreement. It occurs when two or more persons expressly seek to reach an uncoerced agreement about their common situation in order to co-operate and co-ordinate their efforts. This is how Habermas defines it:

Finally the concept of *communicative action* refers to the interaction of at least two subjects capable of speech and action who establish interpersonal relations (whether by verbal or by extra-verbal means). The actors seek to reach an understanding about the action situation and their plans of action in order to coordinate their actions by way of agreement.[18]

As a type of social action, communicative action allows us to envision a human society built on freedom, namely, by the uncoerced co-ordination of the actions of human agents.

To follow further Habermas's thought, he investigates what is meant by rationality in the context of communicative action. He argues that when speakers engage in communicative action their speech acts always raise three validity-claims. These are the claim to truth, the claim to normative legitimacy and the claim to truthfulness or authenticity. These claims may be taken for granted and accepted without question by the actors involved, but their rationality is determined by the willingness of those who make them to engage in argumentation with others to vindicate or criticize those claims when challenged and rendered problematic. Only if speakers are willing to justify their validity-claims in argumentation, namely, a form of discourse in which validity-claims are thematized and reasons given for them, can there emerge a rationally motivated agreement, a rational consensus, on how to co-ordinate actions.

Habermas's concept of communicative rationality, first,

---

[18] Habermas, *The Theory of Communicative Action*, vol. I: *Reason and the Rationalization of Society* (Boston: Beacon Press, 1984), p. 86.

widens the scope of rationality by not confining it to assertions of constative utterances, but applying it also to normative and expressive utterances. He writes:

> In contexts of communicative action, we call someone rational not only if he is able to put forward an assertion and, when criticized, to provide grounds for it by pointing to appropriate evidence, but also if he is following an established norm and is able, when criticized, to justify his action by explicating the given situation in the light of legitimate expectations. We even call someone rational if he makes known a desire or an intention, expresses a feeling or a mood, shares a secret, confesses a deed etc., and is then able to reassure critics in regard to the revealed experience by drawing practical consequences from it and behaving consistently thereafter.[19]

Second, as is clear from the above quotation, communicative rationality for Habermas is bound up with the differentiation of the three classes of validity-claims: truth, normative legitimacy and truthfulness. All three are raised with every speech act, though only one is explicit, with the other two implicit, in each of the three kinds of speech acts. Truth is the explicit claim of assertions or constative utterances; rightness that of normative utterances; and truthfulness the claim of expressive acts.

A third feature of Habermas's account of communicative rationality is that for persons to behave rationally, they must be ready to submit their validity-claims to argumentation, so that the claims can be criticized through arguments and vindicated, if possible, by reasons, reasons of sufficient strength to convince the participants in the argumentation and motivate them to accept the claims. It is the contention of Habermas that all three kinds of validity-claims are open to argumentation and thus to vindication or criticism through reasons.

Before we ask whether the widening of the concept of rationality from a narrow instrumental or strategic rationality to a communicative rationality enables us to determine the rationality of hope, two further points need to be made about Habermas's theory.

Is the theory of communicative action to be regarded as a universally valid, independent ahistorical framework and hence as providing an absolute philosophical grounding for the set of cultural values constituting enlightenment as opposed to mystification, and emancipation as opposed to subjugation? If the answer is yes, Habermas's theory would be an instance of foundationalism. He has, however, constantly denied that interpretation. He understands his theory as replacing Kantian foundationalist epistemology with reconstructive science. Reconstructive science translates the how-to knowledge of competent actors into a how-that knowledge, but the reconstructive efforts remain open to revision. The validity of the reconstructions is to be sought in their fruitfulness as hypothesis in research programmes. To seek in Habermas's theory some absolute grounding for propositional truths or practical norms or values is to interpret the theory against his intentions. Although he claims that the modern understanding of the world and its associated values are of universal significance, he does not give them an absolute status. There is no Absolute Knowledge or Absolute Value, at least for human rationality and discourse.

The second point to be made is that communicative rationality is a procedural concept of rationality, and yet at the same time it does carry with it a content of substantive connotations. The opposition set up by Max Weber between substantive and formal rationality is a false alternative. 'Its underlying assumption is that the disenchantment of religious–metaphysical world views robs rationality, along with the contents of tradition, of all substantive connotations and thereby strips it of its power to have a structure-forming influence on the lifeworld beyond the purposive–rational organization of means.'[20] That assumption is wrong. True, according to Habermas, communicative reason is 'disburdened of all religious and metaphysical mortgages',[21] but, despite its formal character, it is still involved in social life-processes, in so far as the network of communicative actions is the medium in which concrete forms of life are reproduced. The relation between the limits imposed upon communicative

[20] Habermas, *The Philosophical Discourse of Modernity* (Cambridge: Polity Press, 1987), pp. 315–16.
[21] *Ibid.*, p. 316.

reason because of its procedural character and the substantive content inherent in its structure is set out clearly in this passage of Habermas's 'A reply to my critics':

To be sure, the concept of communicative rationality does contain a utopian perspective; in the structures of undamaged intersubjectivity can be found a necessary condition for individuals reaching an understanding among themselves without coercion, as well as for the identity of an individual coming to an understanding with himself or herself without force. However, this perspective comprises *only* formal determinations of the communicative infrastructure of *possible* forms of life and life-histories; it does not extend to the concrete shape of an exemplary life-form or a paradigmatic life-history. Actual forms of life and actual life-histories are embedded in unique traditions. Agnes Heller is right to insist that communication free of domination can count as a necessary condition for the 'good life' but can by no means replace the historical articulation of a felicitous form of life.[22]

There is, then, a telos in communicative action, an inherent orientation to an uncoerced intersubjective understanding and agreement, which grounds the objective possibility of forms of life that would actualize the values implicit in authentic intersubjectivity. This is another way of expressing what was maintained through the concept of the ideal speech situation. It was argued that communicative action contained an implicit reference to discourse or argumentation and to a discursively achieved consensus. Discourse presupposed the ideal speech situation, because it presupposed that an uncoerced agreement was possible. An ideal speech situation was one free from domination, where the only force was the forceless force of the better argument. In its turn the ideal speech situation antici-pated an ideal form of social life, where freedom and responsi-bility were possible.[23]

Habermas will not allow that communicative rationality is a particular option on which we may decide when instead we might choose strategic rationality with its orientation, not to understanding but to success, or make no choice at all, but

---

[22] Thompson and Held, eds., *Habermas: Critical Debates*, p. 228.
[23] Cf. my analysis in Charles Davis, *Theology and Political Society* (Cambridge: Cambridge University Press, 1980), pp. 91–5.

simply follow drives, emotions or habits. Against Heller he writes:

Whenever speaking and acting subjects want to arrive purely by way of argument at a decision concerning contested validity-claims of norms or statements, they cannot avoid having recourse, intuitively, to foundations that can be explained with the help of the concept of communicative rationality. Participants in discourse do not have to come first to an agreement about this foundation: indeed, a decision for the rationality inherent in linguistic understanding is not even possible. In communicative rationality we are always already orientated to those validity-claims, on the intersubjective recognition of which possible consensus depends.[24]

Only from the standpoint of the individual actor can the possibility of such a choice be supposed. But the possibility remains abstract, because from the standpoint of the life-world to which the actor belongs the modes of action envisioned are simply not at one's disposal. The life-world can be reproduced only through the medium of action orientated to reaching understanding.

Of what relevance to religious hope is that lengthy analysis of communicative rationality? Well, at least in the Catholic tradition, there has always been a concern to relate Christian faith, hope and charity to reason and its demands. Although faith, hope and charity establish a transcendent relationship beyond the range of reason, they do so, not by contradicting or violating reason and its criteria, but by opening reason without restriction to the dynamism of the questions reason raises but cannot answer. The widening of the concept of rationality by Habermas against an exclusively instrumental or strategic conception offers theologians the opportunity of re-examining the rational underpinning of the distinctively religious attitudes, granted that Habermas himself does not follow that path.

What are the precise validity-claims made by religious hope? Religious hope is distinguished from the many other varieties of hope by being a total hope. There are innumerable partial hopes cherished by human beings. These tend to coalesce and

---

[24] Thompson and Held, eds., *Habermas: Critical Debates*, p. 227.

form unified and total hope. Such a total hope presupposes a religious understanding of the universe and of human existence. As a multi-dimensional attitude, not a single act, religious hope explicitly raises all three kinds of validity-claim.

Let me begin with the expressive function of hope, that is, with hope as the expression – linguistic, bodily, behavioural, affective and emotional – of the inner conviction, stance and mood of a subject. The validity-claim made by hope as expression is a claim to truthfulness, sincerity, authenticity. To ground such a claim means, in Habermas's phrase, 'establishing the transparency of self-presentations'.[25] How does one do that if the claim is challenged? Here, although there is a move to a reflective level and reasons are put forward, so that one can speak of argumentation in a wider sense, the appeal of argument does not operate in the same straightforward fashion as with the other two validity-claims. First, consistency of behaviour is the key criterion in determining sincerity, rather than argument. Second, in many respects, the greater problem is not the deliberate deception of others concerning one's inner convictions and feelings, but self-deception. In which case, the appropriate procedure is 'therapeutic dialogue or critique', which means psychotherapy for the individual and ideology critique where there is mass delusion. But therapeutic dialogue deviates from the model of argumentation in the strict sense because it does not fulfil the canon of reciprocity, demanding equal shares in the argument for all participants.

Few would deny that religious hope is an area of human experience and history riddled with deception, both of oneself and of others. There is no need to argue with Freud and others who reduce religious hope without remainder to an illusionary formation to acknowledge the necessity of a therapeutic critique to purify religious hope from neurotic and ideological elements. To carry out such a critique is beyond the scope of this programmatic essay with its formal approach, but let me just mention some concrete instances of the corruption I have in mind. There is the murky history of millenarianism. There is

[25] Habermas, *The Theory of Communicative Action*, vol. I: *Reason and the Rationalization of Society*, p. 39.

the use of religious hope as a compensation to legitimate social oppression and injustice. There are the many ways in which people deny death and pretend that the irremovable negativities of human existence can be ignored. The pretence causes distortions in both individual and social existence.

A second validity-claim made by Christian hope is that of rightness or normative legitimacy. This concerns hope as practical, namely, in so far as it is an attitude of confidence governing action and leading one to work for a better world to come, with the norms and values that implies. To ground normative statements means establishing the acceptability of actions or norms of action. When challenged, that acceptability is established by discourse or argumentation, directed towards achieving an uncoerced consensus.

Normative rightness is not a purely individual affair but is to be established with reference to a community or network of intersubjective relationships. The rightness, therefore, of a particular version of Christian hope has, at a first level, to be established with reference to the traditional norms of the historical Christian community. However, at the present time, the interpretation of Christian hope has come under question within the Christian community itself. The rise of Liberation Theology and of political theology, the Marxist and Freudian critiques of religion, the philosophical reaction against Cartesianism and Idealism: these and other developments have brought into the open the tension in the Christian tradition between what may very roughly be designated as the other-worldly and this-worldly interpretations of Christian salvation. Christians themselves are divided in determining the relation between hope for the Kingdom of God and hope for political and social justice and peace. A first requirement of rationality is that such differences should be submitted to argumentation or discourse among those committed to a Christian position. Attempts to establish a consensus by coercive measures is in effect a demand that Christians should cease to be rational in becoming believers.

However, the requirements of rationality in regard to normative claims are not met by ensuring unconstrained discourse within a particular community – here the Christian community – about the interpretation of its own tradition. According to Habermas, norms at the level of morality, as distinct from aesthetic preference, have to have the quality of fairness or impartiality, which implies some version of the principle of universalization. I cannot enter here into the debates about the principle of universalization nor into a discussion of Habermas's claim that it can be rationally justified.[26] I will simply give his version of the principle and indicate its relevance to the grounding of Christian hope. This is how he formulates the principle:

A norm of action has validity only if all those possibly affected by it (and by the side-effect of its application) would, as participants in a practical discourse, arrive at a (rationally motivated) agreement that the norm would come into (or remain) in force, that is, that it should obtain (retain) social validity.[27]

If one accepts that principle, some forms of Christian hope, far from being capable of rational justification, offend against a rational ethic. Religious exclusiveness that puts all who differ outside the realm of salvation is immoral and has inevitably led to patently immoral consequences, such as hatred, cruelty, oppression and injustice. Doctrines of predestination that arbitrarily divide the human race into the elect and the reprobate undermine the basis of rational moral action. Granted the transcendent dimension of eschatological hope, it cannot be allowed to destroy the basis for a rational social morality. To reject concrete groups of people as children of darkness or under some other designation would do so. Eschatological norms and values must be open to rational critique.

The last validity-claim raised by religious hope is to the truth of its assertions. These assertions can be reduced to two. The first affirms the objective possibility, the second the future actuality of the object of hope. The affirmations are grounded

[26] Cf. the discussion of the principle of universalization in Stephan K. White, *The Recent Work of Jürgen Habermas: Reason, Justice and Modernity* (Cambridge: Cambridge University Press, 1987), pp. 48 ff.
[27] Thompson and Held, eds., *Habermas: Critical Debates*, p. 257.

by finding reasons sufficient to establish the existence, present or future, of the state of affairs they respectively describe.

If the object of hope is a just and emancipated society, a social and political life of freedom, reciprocity and shared responsibility, then an orientation towards that goal is, according to Habermas's analysis, indelibly written into the very structure of communicative action. We are inevitably as social subjects engaged in communicative action. As participants in communicative action we cannot but affirm, in performance if not in words, the norms and values of communicative rationality. Because of that, we are justified in seeing our hope for an emancipated society, not as a figment of wishful thinking, but as an intrinsic possibility of our actual situation.

However, that does not of itself justify us in affirming the actual future of an emancipated society. The possibilities inherent in human action may be, and in fact constantly are, frustrated by the negative contingencies of human existence, notably sickness and death and irrational human evil. Secular hope without religion cannot affirm future fulfilment, even partial, with certitude, however promising the present, but must be content with degrees of probability. As for the negative contingencies outside of human control we are left to 'live disconsolately with them'.[28]

At this point we meet religious hope. Religious hope is total, because it is not content to affirm the possibility and future actuality of a destiny proportionate to human beings as fallible, temporal, earth-bound beings, subject to moral failure and death. It discerns in the ordinarily hidden depths of human existence a relation with a transcendent source or power. Through that transcendent relationship human beings are enabled to overcome the otherwise irremovable negativities they confront and reach a fulfilment no longer subject to decay or frustration.[29]

How can such a hope be rationally grounded, given that by definition its object is not proportionate to human existence

---

[28] Jürgen Habermas, *Legitimation Crisis* (London: Heinemann, 1976), p. 120.

[29] The immediate reference of my remarks is Christian hope. However, much of what I say can be applied to other religions.

and, consequently, to human reason? In answering that question it is first necessary to point out that to affirm a transcendent destiny for human beings does not require one to claim any knowledge of the concrete form of that destiny. It is enough to affirm that there is a final fulfilment, that death will be overcome, that injustice will come to an end, that earthly horror will not have the last word, and so on. Descriptive accounts should be interpreted as symbolic expressions of a dynamic orientation to a transcendent power, not as factual assertions.

The rational grounding of the assertion of a possible final fulfilment proceeds from both positive and negative considerations. Positively, there is the consideration that reason, although limited in its temporal embodiment, is of itself an unrestricted dynamism to truth and goodness. Underlying its pursuit of particular truths is a relation to all truth. Its apprehension of particular realities is an openness to universal reality. While the ultimate fulfilment hoped for is not within the range of possibilities proportionate to human reality, the essential openness of reason to all truth constitutes a receptivity to an empowerment from a transcendent source – a receptivity conceptualized by the Scholastics as an obediential potency. Negatively, there is the consideration, urged by Peukert,[30] that communicative action confronts us with the boundary experience of the death of the innocent partner. Those with whom we are in a free, responsible, reciprocal and unconstrained intersubjective relationship through communicative action are arbitrarily removed by death from the communicative relationship. Death destroys the solidarity created by communicative solidarity and renders it nugatory. The fact of death, therefore, creates an aporia for those who affirm communicative action with its distinctive rationality and with its norms and values. That aporia is impassible without appeal to religious tradition. As I wrote, summarizing Peukert's thesis:

---

[30] Helmut Peukert, *Science, Action, and Fundamental Theology* (Cambridge, MA: MIT Press, 1986). Cf. the analysis and discussion of Peukert's thesis in Davis, *Theology and Political Society*, pp. 146–9.

To affirm communicative action as an irreducible and indispensable element of human existence without evading the fact of death or falling into self-contradiction is to affirm the presence of a reality that saves from death and thus discloses itself in human solidarity. In brief, it is to affirm God as the Judaeo-Christian tradition presents him.[31]

To make the argument one for a specific religious tradition is, I think, to go beyond what can reasonably be urged. All the same, the main contention is clear: one cannot consistently take a stand for communicative rationality and ignore the aporia created by the destruction of communication by death.

So far I have been considering only the affirmation of the possibility, not of the future actuality, of an ultimate fulfilment of human needs and desires. However, the appeal to a transcendent source or power underwrites not only the possibility but also the future actuality, together with a present anticipation, of that ultimate fulfilment, the object of human hope. According to the Christian tradition, that actuality comes as a gift or grace. It cannot be inferred as a fact by inspecting the immanent dynamic of human existence and human reason. It is contingent with the gratuitousness of a gift. But without the gift what would have been the solution to the aporias of human existence? Christian thinkers have found it difficult to avoid contradiction here. It is a question of affirming both the gratuitousness and fulfillingness of the object of hope.

One point is clear: the affirmation of the future actuality of what is hoped for – which is the chief cognitive element in the attitude of hope – must be grounded upon an event of a divine disclosure or experience of the Transcendent. As a contingent gift the fact of final fulfilment has to be guaranteed by a revelatory event. In biblical language that revelatory event or series of events is designated as the divine promise. Christian hope is therefore grounded upon the divine promise as declared in a series of events, serving as the vehicle of an experience of the divine reality. The divine promise is not made immediately to individuals as individuals. They are events creative of community, and it is through the community they found that hope is mediated to individuals.

[31] Davis, *Theology and Political Society*, p. 148.

The revelatory events that ground Christian hope are at the same time the founding of a new level of community, namely, a community built upon a shared experience of the Transcendent. Even though it introduces a new level of communicative action, that community is not exempt from following the norms and values of all communicative action, and thus meeting the requirements of a communicative rationality.

We have moved far from the concerns of Habermas and into a theological realm where I strongly doubt he would wish to follow. But theologians have their own preoccupations, and they have in the past not hesitated to exploit the findings of secular knowledge for their own purposes. Habermas's widening of the concept of rationality and his stress upon reason as communicative offer theologians the opportunity of revising their conception of the relation between reason and the Christian life of faith, hope and charity, helping them to overcome the intimidation and distortions of a narrowly conceived positivistic reason.

Index

action, dialectic of, 7–10
Adorno, Theodor, 188, 189
Alves, Ruben, 188, 192
Augustine, 56–7, 66; on original sin, 32, 168

Bauer, Bruno, 83
Baumgartner, Hans Michael, 101–5
Begin, Menachem, 112
Bell, Daniel, 15
Bellah, Robert, 26, 28, 29–30
Benjamin, Walter, 71
Benne, Robert, 179, 186
Bentham, Jeremy, 64
Berger, Peter, 176, 180, 186
bio-power, 162
Bloch, Ernst, 188, 191
Blondel, Maurice, 6–13, 92–5; and William James, 93–4
Bonhoeffer, Dietrich, 40
Boniface VIII, 113
Burke, Edmund, 66–7; his law: revolution leads to tyranny via anarchy, 66

Cieszkowski, August von, 82
communicative action, 150, 157, 194–5
communicative rationality, 194–5, 197; and death, 18
consciousness, philosophy of, 153–4, 156–7
continuity, 100–1; given with narrative construction, 101; not to be identified with temporal duration, 101
Cox, Harvey, 39–40, 80
critical theory, 14

Danto, A., 102–4
death and human communication, 151
deconstructionism, 154–5, 167
DeLubac, Henri, 11
democratic capitalism, 175–81; Christian capitalism an oxymoron, 179
Derrida, Jacques, 154
Descartes, R., 56; Cartesian subject, 56, 194
Dumont, Louis, 45–6

Engels, F., 78
epistemological crisis, 106
evolution, social, 29–30

Feuerbach, Ludwig, 44, 78, 80, 81, 86
Fichte, J. G., 153
finitude, experience of, 53
Flechtheim, A., 17
Foucault, Michel, 159–69; does not favour paradigm of liberation, 164; agonism, *rapport à soi*, 164–5; *exomologesis, exagoreusis*, 166; Foucault and negative theology, 162–9; triangle of knowledge, power and self, 159; proclamation of death of man, 160–2; attitude to power not merely negative, 163
Frankfurt School, 23

Gauchet, Marcel, 3, 5, 41–7
genealogy, 162, 165
Gilby, Thomas, 33
Glazer, Nathan, 15
Glotz, Peter, 15
Gogarten, F., 4, 80

206

Habermas, Jürgen, 14–16, 25, 26, 34, 156–7, 169, 189–91, 194–5, 199, 205; Baumgartner and Danto on historical knowledge, 101–5; on post-modernity, 155–7
Hegel, G. F. W., 153
Hegelianism, Marx on, 78
Heller, Agnes, 189, 197
history, three essential features: retrospectivity, constructivity, practical interest, 101
hope, its presuppositions, 191–3; as multi-dimensional 190–3; rationally grounded, 202–5
Horkheimer, Max, 188

ideal speech situation, 197
identity, conventional identity, 135–6; universalistic identity or post-conventional, 136–7
individualism, 45; Christian individualism, 68–9; possessive individualism, 137
intersubjectivity, 169, 197

Jakobson, Roman, 98
James, William, and Blondel, 93
jihad, 113
John XXIII, 39
Kierkegaard, 153
Kohlberg, L., 134
Kolakowski, Leszek, 92, 175, 188
Kristol, Irving, 15

Lamb, Matthew, 178
Leo XIII, 32
Lichtheim, G., 184
Lipset, Seymour Martin, 15
Lobkowicz, Nicholas, 79–80
logocentrism, 155
Lonergan, Bernard, 153, 154, 169
Luther, Martin, 32
Lyotard, Jean-François, 155

MacIntyre, Alasdair, 106–9
MacPherson, C. B., 137
MacQuarrie, John, 192–3
Maritain, Jacques, 112
Marx, Karl, 78; Marxist critique of religion, 79; relation of theory and *praxis* in Marx, 81–5; on ideology, 85

Merton, Thomas, 132
metaphysics of presence, 155
Metz, J. B., 188
Milbank, John, 1, 6, 11–13, 17
Mill, John Stuart, 64
modernity, 1, 23, 124; ambiguity of, 23; as autonomous self-consciousness, 24; contrast with traditional societies as transition from mythos to logos, 25; incompatible with religion, 26, 30; project of, 156
Moltmann, Jürgen, 188
Murray, John Courtney, 33–5

narrative, two levels: narratives produced by participants and narratives constructed by historians, 105; history must retain a narrative form, 105
neo-conservatism, 14–15
Newman, John Henry, 100–1, 169
Nicholls, David, 114, 115
Nietzsche, F. W., 157
nihilism, 36
Nisbet, Robert, 15
non-violence, 46–7
Novak, Michael, 15–17, 173–87

Panikkar, Raimundo, 127, 132
phonocentrism, 155
pluralism, 28–9, 33–4
positivism, 26–8, 85–7; associated in theology with Karl Barth, 86; coincides with dogmatism, 85
post-modernity, 41, 153–69
post-structuralism, 154
pure nature, concept of, 10–11

radicalism, 5–6, 63–73; contrast with Christian faith, 65–73; and egalitarianism, 71–2; three elements of, 63–5
Rahner, Karl, 88
rationality, of sciences dependent upon narrative, 106; rationality proper to tradition consists in an openness to development, 109
reconstructive science, 196
reductionism, 29
relativism, 28
religion, as a form of social practice, 2; as a social system, not to be

identified with interiority, 49; not a
distinct cultural sphere, 51–5;
religion of inwardness, three modes
of religion: cosmic, contemplative,
political, 55–8; Marxist critique of,
79; religion and politics, 119–21
religious faith, awareness of
Transcendent, 35; distinction
between faith and belief, 35; as
revolutionary, rejects all
absolutism, 37–8
religious language, 112–19
revelation, 96–100; as verbal
communication, 98; concept of, 108
Ryle, Gilbert, distinction between
achievement verbs and task
verbs, 96

Schelling, F. W. J., 189
Schelsky, H., 189
Schumacher, E. F., 22
secular, 5; as context for theology, 6
secularization, 1; theology of, 40, 80
Shils, Edward, 15
social evolution, four stages of, 145–8
socialism, as a political vision, 173;
assumption of Christian socialism,
181–3; movement for a new social
order, 183; socialism as rejection of
wage relationship, 183–4
society, secular, 2; modern, 2; as an
artefact, 2; cannot rest on empirical
sciences alone, 31; role of religious
faith, 37; sacral, secular and

pluralist societies, *halakhic* society,
121–3; modern society as product
of free human agency, 124
structuralism, 154; Foucault rejects
designation 'structuralist', 154–8
supernatural, 10; and the dialectic of
human action, 10; necessary idea of
supernatural, 10

Taylor, Barbara, 174
Taylor, Mark C., 17
theologies of mediation, 87
Thomism, 153
Thompson, E. P., 183–6
three spheres of value or realms of
meaning: cognitive, normative,
expressive, 49
tradition, constituted by conflict of
interpretation, 107–8

Unger, Roberto Mangabeira, 1, 21, 22,
23, 24, 27, 29
universalism, 133; and religious identity,
136–9

validity – claims, three classes: truth,
normative legitimacy, truthfulness,
194–5; made by religious hope,
198
Vatican II, 40

Weber, Max, 25
Wellmer, A., 91
Westcott, B. F., 183

CAMBRIDGE STUDIES IN IDEOLOGY
AND RELIGION

Books in the series

*A Theology of Reconstruction: Nation-Building
and Human Rights*
CHARLES VILLA-VICENCIO

Christianity and Politics in Doe's Liberia
PAUL GIFFORD

Protestantism in Contemporary China
ALAN HUNTER AND KIM-KWONG CHAN

Politics, Theology, and History
RAYMOND PLANT

Christianity and Democracy: A Theology for a Just World Order
JOHN W. DE GRUCHY

Pastoral Care and Liberation Theology
STEPHEN PATTISON

Religion and the Making of Society: Essays in Social Theology
CHARLES DAVIS